Living a Passionate Life!

Sofia Michaels

Living a Passionate Life!

Copyright © 2013 by Sofia Michaels

All rights reserved by the author. No part of this publication may be reproduced, stored in a retrieval system or transmitted in any form or electronic, mechanical, photocopying, recording or otherwise, without the prior written permission of the author. Karma is always in effect. For more information, please write: Street Smart Publishing, 8526 Stonebrook Circle, Middleton, WI 53562.

Street Smart Publishing paperback edition published 2013.

Street Smart Publishing electronic edition published 2013.

Proudly printed in the United States of America.

ISBN 13: 978-0-615-88743-2

Notice: This book is a call to no longer be afraid of life, but rather learn to embrace life fully and get the real experience you were supposed to have here on Earth. You can only do that by diving in. People who tip-toe into the water might be happy, but people who dive right in know passion.

This book isn't for people looking to discover their passion and purpose in life. It's for people who already know their passion and want to be inspired to take it further, or perhaps voyeurs who want to get a front-row seat to peek intimately at passion in action as they have never seen it before.

Also by Sofia Michaels

Pretendia: Smash the Glass Slipper and Awaken Your Best Self

Hiding in Plain Sight

By Sheri Fermanich

Personally Branded

Priceless Asset$

Table of Content

Lesson 1 – Foreplay!..9
Lesson 2 – Living a Passionate Life! 33
Lesson 3 – Living a Dirty Life!.....................................58
Lesson 4 – Living La Vida Loca! 85
Lesson 5 – Experiencing Life! 111
Lesson 6 – Make it a Great Day! 137
Lesson 7 – Passion Workers! 161
Lesson 8 – Family Legacy! 189
Lesson 9 – Having Fun! 221
Lesson 10 – Almost Heaven! 246
Photography Credits..273
Acknowledgements...275
About the Author 277

Dedicated to Andre Michaels, my husband, of 18 years:

Since the day I saw you wearing a tuxedo in the church basement at your sister's wedding, there has been a sacred space that only you and I have been to that means the world to me. You are the man who gave me my life's highest dream – our three children. With all the ups and downs of a real extraordinary life, we always hang on to our dynamic connection with fierce loyalty.

Love,
Spicy Salsa

Life's profound experience is up to you.

– Sofia Michaels

Lesson 1
Foreplay!

I've never seen so many trees in my life in such breath-taking deep greens. The abundant nature you could see for miles heightened my essence and "a-ha" moments about life all week while my husband Andre and I had been on vacation. From the healing springs at The Jefferson Bath House that left me more relaxed and sedated on the front porch of The Homestead since before I had children, to the Gorge Hike with Brian and gorgeous waterfall after waterfall that made me want to cry they were so beautiful, my life changed here in so many visceral ways.

Every inch of my being felt heightened and aware.

The final morning of our vacation, I stepped out onto the veranda and took a gorgeous breath of fresh air where the glistening sun touched my face like a warm, soft kiss and I felt it. Suddenly, the most amazing sensation came all through my body. It started in my chest like an exciting impulse, and traveled quickly to a tingling of goose-bump explosions down both arms and rocketed through my legs and out my toes.

I knew exactly what was happening. I have experienced this amazing feeling so many times before over the last three years. The experience has always left a warm smile on my face that I have never shared with anyone else before, not even Andre.

"What's happening?" Andre, my husband, asked, as I remembered I wasn't alone. I had to giggle to myself with embarrassment.

"Something is happening. I can see it on your face. Tell me what's happening," Andre gently pried. My heart was pounding as I said nothing. "I've seen this look before" he added.

Oh, I feared I was going to be in trouble with Andre and I didn't know how I could avoid it. He was standing right there in front of me and had seen the whole thing happen with his own eyes. *Think fast. What should I say?* I had promised Andre I wouldn't write another book so soon. But it was stronger than me. It came on so quickly it took over my senses, especially my mind.

I took a deep breath. Slowly I turned to face Andre. *What could I possibly say that he could understand?*

"I know I promised you I wouldn't start to write a new book right away, I said I'd market *Pretendia* first. I tried to not think about a new book. Honestly, I did. I tried to mind my own business, but it... it..." My voice trailed off. *Andre had every right to be annoyed with me.*

Andre gently put his hands on my shoulders and softly, said "Did you just get an idea for a new book?" I took one step closer to him, looked deep into his eyes, praying he'd understand. "Yes," I managed to whisper as I leaned into his chest and kept my eyes on his eyes in a "please, please, understand," fashion.

Andre amazed me when he said, "I don't understand this at all, this writing thing. But I can see it makes you very happy. So do what you need to do."

Maybe it was all perfectly timed, since he was in the most relaxed, loving mood from a week of vacation. But he had just essentially told me,

"Go after your passion. I release you from the deal you made as I can see you aren't able to keep it, in spite of wanting to."

I had just finished my fifth book in five years. Andre had always been supportive of my writing. Yet, at times it felt like I was having an emotional affair in our marriage. I wrote everywhere I could – at home, at the gym, on family trips, at 5 a.m. And Andre had his own "mistress," too, that took his time, attention, and physical presence away from me too. You'll hear more about that in a moment.

We were at a crossroads in our marriage. We realized we both needed to be released to go after our passions that we didn't share – personal development and youth athletics. If we weren't each released to follow our bliss, we might lose our marriage and intimate connection to each other. To many people that may feel threatening and yet, we both knew we had to or we would lose the wonderful part of each of our spirits. That meant we had to accept and be willing to allow what is perhaps the best part of ourselves to be experienced outside of our marriage, with other people.

Living a Passionate Life!

Who does this in a marriage and decides that is acceptable? Or maybe more people should.

Unshared passion tends to be a fighting topic among couples. It's understandable. The raw reason tends to be scarcity. People fight because of limited resources such as time, money, attention, or connection. We want our partner's attention, time, and connection. Maybe there's not enough time for me and you to enjoy our passions, so someone misses out or it's a bitter fight to the end – who ends up getting to enjoy their passion, and who ends up with the short end of the stick again.

It can be hard to negotiate amicably to come up with a way that you can both be happy. It can be jealous and combative until you figure out a way to do it better. Maybe one of you is full of passion, and one of you seems passionless. This can cause another level of jealousy and conflict, as the one without passion desperately wants it, but try as she might, she can't even muster the beginning flint of a passion flame which makes her feel like she doesn't want you to have it either. As you read this you may react defensively and think, "I would never do that to my partner!" But it happens every day for certain couples.

In the past, Andre and I struggled to accommodate our separate passions. It wasn't that we had a problem with one another's passion.

As a writer with three children, a husband and two dogs, Fiesta and Jose, I have adapted my schedule in order to find time to write. I get up at 5 a.m. every day and write until 7 a.m. and am in bed by 8:30 p.m. or 9:00 p.m. That leaves night owl Andre up without a partner too as he gets up in just enough time to get to work in the morning.

Andre's passion is coaching youth athletics. People

frequently would say to me, "At least he's not in a bar." True, I would not be with him if that was the case. But I still feel it when he's not home six nights per week. As a sports widow I am left to do all of the heavy lifting of being married, with little benefit, for nine months out of every year.

During our wedding ceremony Father Charlie said directly to me, "There are four seasons in the Michaels family; basketball, basketball, basketball, basketball." Fifteen years and three children later, when Father Charlie was retiring, I wrote him to congratulate him and said, "After fifteen games, ten practices and nine loads of laundry this week, I now know what you were saying to me during our wedding ceremony. Every day I pray for patience. Please pray for me." It gave Father Charlie a good laugh, and I'm sure it's a story to tell when he counsels couples.

The years when the children were little were the hardest – we were both tired, stretching every dollar as far as we could and putting all of our time and attention into Mia, Dante, and Lexi. Neither of us was getting much personal passion back then. We did manage a few hours a week, but we both would have liked more. Believe me, they were worth it and we knew we were building a foundation in those years, but it was still tough on a daily basis.

Today we are at an easy stage. Mia is 16 and a sophomore in high school. A classic first-born, she's had her sights set on college since middle school. She loves school and has big goals for herself. Mia is strong-willed, has a fire in her belly like me, and has the same sense of humor and passion for athletics like her dad. Mia has my dark hair, olive skin color and brown eyes, yet looks the most like her dad.

Dante is 14 and fabulously atypical for a teenage boy. He gets his homework done without being asked, lets me hug him before school every day, and he's kind to both of his sisters. He is self-motivated as well, and has set some amazing challenges for himself, including high-level athletics. Dante looks more like me at this age and is logical, neat and particular like his dad.

Lexi is 12 and a great student, too. She's into making movies, creative projects, and babysitting. Her personality and creativity resembles me. In her organization and logical decision-making, she's like her dad. Lexi looks just like me except for her dad's lighter skin color and hair, with her paternal grandpa's blue eyes.

All of them can cook, do laundry, clean, grocery shop with an eye for value, and do yard work. They don't fight when they are home alone because we don't allow it. And Mia is driving now, which makes our activity schedule easier.

Andre and I both realize we are at a new stage in our lives now. We are needed emotionally by Mia, Dante and Lexi, but less physically than when they were little. We are both aware that we need our own lives too – it can't all be about the children. When they leave home, we want to still feel happy and fulfilled. You'll hear more about our passion for parenting in lesson eight.

As we are almost down the mountain, leaving The Homestead behind, I glance to my left at just the exact moment to see a street sign that says "Almost Heaven." Another wave of excitement passes through my body and I think how wonderful. "Almost Heaven" – that's exactly right. There was definitely something about this experience at The Homestead. It was the most unexpected, relaxing vacation Andre and I have had so far.

Essentially, according to Andre, I am free now to surrender to as much bliss as I want in my life. I've never had that luxury before. You would think unlimited happiness is an easy thing to accept. What wife wouldn't want the green light from her spouse to go make herself as happy as she would like? For me, it's not that easy. It wasn't like I wasn't happy already. I have had plenty of happiness in my life and am grateful for all of it. What I would not allow myself to do is embrace happiness completely without being guarded.

For most of my life, I've had a fear of enjoying my life "too much." There was always an imaginary line I wouldn't cross, no matter how badly I wanted to. That sounds absurd, so let me explain. I believed if I was "too happy," and people are aware of it, it would all be taken away from me. *Be cautious with happiness* was the thought that was always in the back of my mind. I thought that fear was not normal. But it has haunted me intensely for more than half my life.

It started when my first serious boyfriend, Stephan, was killed in a car accident by his good friend, a drink driver. I was seventeen. The first thing my grandmother said to me when I saw her was, "Be careful how happy you are or it will all be taken away."

At that immature age, and in the face of gut-wrenching pain, I knew for certain I never wanted to feel such pain again. My grandmother's words entered my mind and stayed deep. I knew her son had died in a car accident at 21, and she was still mad at God about it. Knowing why she said what she did didn't lessen its affect on me.

When Andre and I first got married, and especially when we had little children, I'd worry if he was even five minutes late from work. At 15 minutes late, if he hadn't called me, I was sure he had been in a car accident. Luckily, we both survived my neurotic behavior. I'm long since over it. And yet, for almost 20 years I haven't been able to completely overcome my irrational fear of happiness, and I knew it was time.

Our culture seems to encourage a second caution about happiness. Remember that 1980s shampoo commercial: "Don't hate me because I'm beautiful?" Perhaps it really meant, "Don't hate me because I'm happy." That's the dirty truth of our culture. Just like when we were little, we feared someone might take our toy (happiness) if they see us fully enjoying it. They would want it for themselves. Sadly, some people resent our happiness. So happiness is actually something I've hidden more than I've shared in my life, thinking I had to protect it.

I was promoted early and often in my career. Right away, some didn't like it. Of course, they concluded, it wasn't my own merit that helped me advance. It was my appearance, or ability to "sexually hypnotize any man to do exactly as I please." These were the crazy rumors that flew. My only defense was to work harder.

It's ugly, but you see it all the time. Contemporarily, we call them "haters." They aren't happy in their own lives, so they hate it when anyone else is. These toxic people who gossip, spread lies and generally cause problems for anyone experiencing good fortune. They are the mistresses or misters who ruin families more than marriages. They are the friends who eagerly take in your private information and use it later to sabotage any good feelings you may have had about them and yourself.

By the age of 25, I tended to have males as friends. I

don't seem to threaten them when I win or achieve. They couldn't care less about what I'm wearing, how much I paid for it or if my house was clean. Of course I have female friends. The women I am friends with are happy in their own lives. They are ambitious, supportive, funny, and into personal development. They are wives and mothers. Many are readers and a few even love cheesecake as much as I do. My friends, male or female, are not haters – far from it. They are not self-centered or superficial and interested in making a difference in the world.

I am accountable to myself, not to others. The only productive thing I can do is to address the reasons why, then push myself over the cliff for good. Why make room for more bliss? Because at this level of my personal development, 1) I know I can be happier if I let myself, and 2) I want to test the premise that the purpose of life is to be happy.

The remaining ways I still hold happiness back:

- "Working" all the time. I constantly juggle work and my personal life, rarely relaxing.
- Warrior/defense mindset, too often.
- Worry.
- Must do everything in one big huge action (too impatient for baby steps.)
- Don't take the easy way.
- Always in charge, even when I don't want to.
- Can't relax until...

You see, to this point, I have run and strived for most of my life. I was always trying to get "somewhere" or move my family along in life, a life I had always wanted and barely dared to admit to myself, or publically, I had achieved it. The truth is, I could relax now and enjoy my present moment. But when you've been a striver warrior most of your life, that's easier said than done. Warriors don't sit calmly very often.

Since the age of 17, what I have been the most interested in is personal development. Every day of my life, I have focused on what can I learn today that interests me or how I can become a better person. My interest has always been personal evolution. That intensified in my 40s. Particularly, I was done with physical wants in the world and instead want to fully experience life and give the most back before my timer goes off for good.

Many Americans never get to a place where they are at peace and focused on consciousness, rather than materialism and achievement. Plenty of people in their 80s haven't. However, it is possible at any age to evolve to a consciousness above ego and be happy in the present moment, no matter what else is happening in your life.

In Western culture, there are three main teachings that come from our egos that can cause major chaos with our happiness and passion as well as our real purpose here on earth. Author and speaker Wayne Dyer refers to them as "accidental" or false teachings of the ego.

1) I am what I have (materialism, accumulation)
2) I am what I do (job titles, kudos, resume)
3) I am what other people think of me (reputation)

I Am What I Have – In everyday life, you will encounter people who have been taught or who believe that "I am what I have." These people have unhealthy relationships with their possessions. The advertising messages we receive and the easy availability of credit reinforce this misconception. People who believe this judge themselves externally. "Do I drive the right kind of car? Am I dressed better than her? Do I have more toys than him?"

The recent economic bust had a devastating impact on the American ego. Losing possessions for any reason other than choosing to dump them for the next big thing tends to cause many of us a mini depression. To continue to feel superior to others, we must acquire new things all the time. The truth is, we don't even enjoy these items as much as we enjoy other people seeing us with them. We like the feeling we get from having things others do not.

"I am what I have" works the opposite way with ego too, leaving people with a low self-concept thinking, "if I don't have much, I am not worth much." Obviously this accidental teaching does not take into account the true value of a human being.

You can tell if you, or anyone else, believes in this accidental teaching if you hear talk about possessions, trips, and money-dominated opportunities instead of truly connecting as a human being with other human beings. The saddest part of this teaching is that it is such an empty false teaching for wealthy and poor people.

I Am What I Do – This accidental teaching can be learned at a very young age. Were grades, awards, sport trophies, prizes earned for talent, and promotions praised when you were growing up? Are you a former high school or college athlete who feels you experienced a "death" when you could no longer compete at that level? Are you addicted to impressing people with the latest examples of your acumen on the job or the sales trips you've won? Are you a PTO (Parent Teacher

Organization) parent who competes to be the most selfless volunteer of the year? Such overachievers even frequent our churches.

When a person bases his or her personal worth on a role like a lawyer, a professional athlete, or company executive, an identity crisis may result if the person loses that role. In Western culture, people are conditioned socially to accept this "I am what I do" philosophy. Think of the first thing that we say when we meet someone: "What do you do?" or "Do you work out of the home?" Without this ice-breaker, it can be hard to get a conversation going. In our society we feel intrusive asking about the self, rather than the external facts of people's lives.

I Am What Other People Think Of Me – We give so much of our power away by believing we are our reputations. Reputation is a false idol. People who worship it say they feel like impostors, or they exhaust themselves trying to keep up the image they so desperately want.

Do you have the same reputation in the privacy of your home with your loved ones as you do in your professional or social life? This is what's really worth caring about.

According to Ramana Maharshi, an Eastern guru, "All unhappiness is due to the ego." The ego is an unfed monster when it comes to reputation. It is insatiable and finicky. We feel fabulous about ourselves when we have a good reputation, depressed when some human error or botched job at work reveals us to be human.

The ironic part is that if we just cared about our soul and not what anyone thought of it, we wouldn't need the devil. Our soul is the authentic reflection of who we really are.

The answer to these three accidental teachings of the ego is to learn to focus on your authentic self and what you want your ideal life to be. Say your friend gets a new car as a bonus from a promotion at work. Can you be genuinely happy for him and not feel differently about yourself after hearing the news. If you feel different about yourself after hearing of your friend's good fortune, it may be your ego getting in the way.

You will discover, when you have let go of the ego's teachings, that living life on your own terms and allowing others to do the same. Gratitude is the source of all happiness. Research tells us happy people are healthier, live longer and do more good for their families, businesses, communities and ultimately, the world. Happiness is a fleeting emotion. But a commitment to the authentic self ensures even stronger happiness.

A big shift seems to be happening in our society right now. Many are rejecting an aimless life for one filled with meaning and purpose. Perhaps this is the best outcome of the Great Recession. People have woken up and want more from life. We can see this in the rise of conscious capitalism and financial literacy, in families spending more quality time together, in new environmental concerns, in the shift in careers from jobs to passion work, and in the political unrest that signals spiritual revolt.

My trip to The Homestead in Virginia viscerally told me that it was time to be fully awake. It was a gargantuan invitation and it came at the perfect time in my life. I was ready. Specifically, I was ready to allow anyone I encounter to know the real me, to trust that it will be to my benefit to do that.

What is passion?

The dictionary defines passion narrowly as:

1. any powerful or compelling emotion or feeling, as love or hate.
2. intense enthusiasm: a strong liking or enthusiasm for a subject or activity.
3. strong sexual desire; lust.
4. the sufferings of Christ on the cross or subsequent to the Last Supper.

Is it possible to be mildly passionate? These definitions suggest otherwise. "Mild" passion is an oxymoron.

When you are passionate you don't tire easily, you lose track of hours, and you wake up eager to do what gives you passion all over again. It becomes your priority, and you'll compromise other things to get more of it. Ironically, passion releases the same feel-good endorphins like dopamine that being in love produces. The after-effect may last for days. You experience a range of emotions: excited, stressed, frustrated, yearning, impulsive, daring, euphoric. Some passions are soft and enjoyable, others large and explosive.

This book focuses on healthy or harmonious passion, which is associated with positive consequences. What it will not promote is obsessive passion, which is associated with negative consequences. How can you tell the difference? It comes down to the intent, quantity and consequences in your life. Passion for parenting, for example, seems like a healthy passion. Yet it depends on the type of parent you are – for example, we know helicopter parents are obsessive and controlling.

Passion is a hot emotion no matter how you look at

it. It's not cold like despise, or mild like happiness. The best way to look at it is by using a hotness scale like Quaker Steak and Lube uses to help you visualize and understand how hot each sauce is for their signature wings, from ranch being the mildest to Triple Atomic being their absolute hottest.

As a reference, happiness would be on the mild end of passion. True, deep, intense passion is on the Triple Atomic end.

Some people seem to be born more passionate than others. For instance, by middle school age I was over flowing with "high energy." I was up at the crack of dawn and spent a good five hours alone before I could call a friend or make plans out of the house. In those five hours a day on weekends or everyday in summer, I busied myself drawing, writing, or playing "apartment" or school with imaginary friends.

I learned early to hide my passion and keep it private. One reason was that my adoptive dad, a computer expert, found my exuberance messy and weird. Creative play seemed to make some people uncomfortable.

As a junior in high school, I was chosen by my peers to run for State DECA President. At the state convention, state officer candidates all had to wear the polyester blue DECA blazer – the ugliest popcorn-textured, boring piece of non-fashion I had encountered in the 80s. *How was I supposed to stand out in that?* I quickly figured it out. I could meet the dress code and still feel like myself if I wore a tight-fitting red mini-skirt with a white lace shirt under the blazer, along with navy blue tights and heels. When I walked on stage, in front of two thousand of my peers, my confidence, red mini-skirt, and swinging hips made a statement. People still talk about that moment today. When I won, for the first time I realized I could completely be myself and people liked it!

My senior year of high school I missed over forty days of school. I traveled the state speaking and presenting, creating and performing skits, executing marketing campaigns, learning to be a good-will ambassador, networking with businesses, leading my fellow state officers, competing in restaurant marketing, and attending DECA Nationals. I had finally found something I loved and was good at. I put everything I had into it. Marketing was a way to use creativity in business that people actually admired. Often, it can take some time or trying different things to grow into your passion.

This is the kind of intensity I put into anything I do. I can't help it. The opposite is also true. If I have no interest, I really can't make myself care. My physical energy is the same way. I only have two speeds – 100 miles an hour or asleep. I was sure that would wear off after middle school, then maybe college, and at 45 it's still true. Maybe it won't disappear until I'm 90.

This might all sound great to you, as you aren't dealing with me in person to feel what it's really like. It's embarrassing, but I've even had close friends say to Andre, "Geez, she talks fast," or "I'm exhausted just watching her." Andre just smiles and says, "Welcome to my world, and she gets up at 4 or 5 a.m.!" I'm just excited and excitable about so many things in life. I'll take this quirky glitch over pessimism any day. I've learned to respect it as the gift it is.

Passion perhaps feels different to different people, much like dancing. There are as many styles of dancing as there are styles of music, and on top of that everyone moves differently to the music. Just watch people dance at a wedding. Some are stiff as a board, some are wild and flailing all over, and others have a hippy vibe. We express passion in much the same way.

Writers and artists, for example, express their love for the craft in a wide variety of ways. When Lexi, my youngest daughter, shows me a painting she's done, I'm always in awe of her talents. One Christmas she went to my mom's to work on a secret project. On Christmas Eve, Andre and I opened a family portrait that Lexi had created. She had painted each member of our family, and for a fun surprise, she had squeezed herself upside down above everyone else. It made me laugh with pleasure. After Christmas, she told me she had run out of room. That's why she added herself upside down, where she found space. She's always so creative. I love it. The painting was extra special because she had created it with her maternal grandma during one of their special craft times.

One non-profit worker may be calm in his perseverance, while another one is pushy and abrasive. A teacher may be strong, strict, and challenging, engaging students and making them require more of themselves. The next teacher may be laid back, easy to relate to and a soft place to fall during the tumultuous years of high school. All of these workers display a passion for their craft in their own way.

None of this means passion is all blissful. It's more like being on a raft: a beautiful sunny day gives you tantalizing sensations, but can also turn into storms. When the storms come in, it may mean that season in your life needs to end due to age, declining ability, or changing circumstances. Other times, even if you feel devastated, you'll find a way to get back on the raft and ride again. Just look at adventurers who suffer near-death experiences. Within months, many are back at the adventure. Something in their spirit and attitude about life refuses to keep them on the couch watching Oprah. It appears they have to go engage fully in life in order to feel alive.

I can never experience the passion Andre feels when he is deep in the middle of coaching a game or intense practice. I can watch him and observe what I think he is feeling, but I can never actually go there with him. The one year I coached, by default, I didn't experience the same thrill. I'm competitive enough that I want to win every time, but I wouldn't call that passion for me.

What is the painter or sculpture thinking as they create a physical object in reality from their mind? I don't know. I wonder, and am intrigued, but I can't enter the sacred door, the one that gives her access to her imagination. So I am left with a flat, one-dimensional experience that I don't find the wonder in.

The actress may call this sacred place "being in character." An athlete refers to it as "being in the zone." But the effect is the same. You lose a sense of reality for a while, floating in euphoria. An author may be unaware of her fingers as they fly across the keys. She may be amazed by what appears on the paper as text. After the fact, her readers can be carried to that place she experienced, to some extent – yet not to the intensity.

In the movie *Flashdance*, the untrained dancer Alex experiences pure joy when she moves. Her boss, Nick, was so attracted to her as he watched her moving and experiencing bliss in every fiber of her being. Then Alex's grandmother died, and he found out that he had pulled strings to get her the audition. Alex told Nick she was not going to audition for the Conservatory. Nick said,

"You're using me as an excuse to not go to the audition. Just know when you stop going after your dream – you die."

Those two points are so valid when it comes to dreams and passion.

1) **You are using something as an excuse to not go after your passion.**

Oh, the bitter sins of a passionate person – the keeper of such a precious gift. We wouldn't dare believe we would sabotage ourselves and the gift. It's human nature at certain points of our journey with passion when we get too scared to take a deep breath and go after it, come what may.

How painful to watch someone sabotage her passion. Like setting a beautiful Steinway grand piano on fire and watching it burn, as you realize you will never be able to play it again. Or letting a competitor steal your business, in an unethical maneuver, while you do nothing but watch them take everything from you.

In this country, we have the constitutional right to pursue happiness. It is not permission to leave your family destitute and go obsess over your dreams. It states the "right to pursue." Pursue is a negotiated term, unless you are absolutely alone, which is very unlikely. "Pursuit of happiness" may mean one thing to a single person and another to a single parent, and yet another thing to a spouse with or without children.

The second part of Nick's warning is equally important.

2) **When you stop going after your dreams – you will die.**

The "you" in the statement refers to your spirit.

Anyone who has tried to stop his or her passion, put it in a drawer for a period of time, or given it up altogether knows what that statement means. You feel lifeless, unmotivated, lost, and aimless. It's a rotten feeling for a passionate person.

At one point in my career as an entrepreneur, I was really being pushed to give it up and I lost my way. I ignored my strong connection to the fact that everything about me points to my spirit is an entrepreneur. I was really being pushed to give up my joy.

Andre wanted me to have a job. He certainly didn't know or understand that my actual spirit would be different if I abandoned my creative dreams. In the end, as I have shared in *Pretendia*, I couldn't do it. It took some serious struggle for me to come to terms with this.

I felt guilty for being "selfish." There was frustration over the economy. I felt angry at my partner for not giving me credit as a parent and a wife, and at myself for not earning so much it didn't matter. I felt sad imagining losing my freedom to be creative and spending my priceless time raising our children. The resolution took compromise, understanding and an upswing in the real estate market.

Andre is a steady man. He has a great job with excellent insurance and receives a steady paycheck. I, on the other hand, may go for months without a paycheck – but when I get one, it's big. Our solution was to reach a place where we have no debt, and Andre's check covers everything essential. I provide my family's "big bang" things – the higher-ticket items.

We have certainly had the same issue over his passion – coaching youth athletics. My problem was not the activity itself, but Andre's obsessiveness – volume, time, money, away from the family – with which he goes about it. It was like being married to The Nutty Professor in the movie *Flubber*. I had to figure out how to get along with three minutes of his attention in a day.

It was not that I couldn't understand he was doing good for our children and in the world. Plenty of people admire Andre.

What helped was knowing that Andre's intense passion will moderate when our children are no longer in middle school. I can't imagine a time when I won't be able to write anymore, or anyone telling me I can't write. That would leave me feeling so empty and unsure as to what I should do with myself in the world. So with more empathy, I stepped back and let him have all the passion he wanted. For six months I said nothing about his coaching.

The interesting part is when I did that, Andre reached his own conclusion about what's too much. I'll never forget the February night when he admitted to me, "It's too much." He was coaching four basketball teams at the same time. I just smiled and said, "I understand." It also helped to realize that when he is at practice, I can enjoy my passion. I have free time to read, write, or go for a walk and think. And I don't have to feel guilty about any of this. So instead of fighting against each other for our passions, I learned to coordinate them as much as I can which helped our marriage improve.

You don't want to ask someone to give up their passion because they are part of a couple. That never goes well for either party.

The truth is we both need our passions, but the

priority is we both want a strong marriage. When you take care of the relationship first, chances are your partner will be more understanding about your passion. Andre and I realize that in seven years we'll be empty-nesters. Neither of us wants to be staring at the other over a salad and have nothing to talk about. So it's imperative we keep our passions and at the same time build a strong relationship that will withstand our children going on to lead their own blissful lives.

Certainly couples exist who have the same passions. They may love rock climbing, building wells in Africa or volunteering at church. Andre and I share a passion for family as well as for education, although we go about these differently. Andre and I may find bliss together later in our lives, when I travel for speaking or he opens an athletic facility.

When I started talking about my idea for this new book, people instantly responded, "Ohhh, I want to read that!" Yet when I began posting deeper thoughts about passion on Facebook, people got uncomfortable. In person, I got the same reactions. People sounded very interested in hearing about the topic and wanted more details. Oddly, the question that made people the most uncomfortable was "What are you fiercely committed to?" They were silent or tried to use humor. Their reactions surprised me, as I didn't even think it was an intimate question. Yet I have to admit, a part of me knows passion makes people uncomfortable. And I get a kick out of making people squirm. I even have a saying for it when I write or say a zinger – "Sass-A-Phrase."

If I were speaking about sexual passion, people would be much more comfortable. The common perception is that non-sexual passion is more intimate than the sexual kind. At first I found that perplexing. Now, I've come to understand it. We are so inundated with sexual messages every day that we become numb to them. However, when it comes to knowing your authentic passion by articulating what gives us joy, many of us refuse to share. It makes us feel "too naked."

We spend so much of our lives being guarded, afraid if I love you completely, you'll hurt me. Cautious to really let someone in when you know they are dying because if you let them into your heart you already know the raw, searing pain you will get in the end. Perhaps we do that with the number of friends we allow in our lives. I'm guilty of that. My friends are few and intimate because of how deep and open those relationships are. I've found few people who can have friends that way. Yet it's what I need and want for emotional connections.

My mom's the one who taught me to be compassionate to the elderly and fully present for people who are dying. She has been "comfortable" with it her whole life. When I was younger it was hard to understand why she would put herself through that gut-wrenching pain. "No one deserves to die alone," was her answer, "That's when they need support the most." I looked at my mom differently after that for her ability to bring joy to people at the end of life.

This caution in life is exactly what keeps us from living a full experience.

Passion isn't about what you have, where you live, what you drive, or who you know. You don't have to have a dollar to be passionate. Passion is a chosen attitude. It's the inner fire (your personal WHY) that propels you forward even when you are not winning.

When things are hard and you think about quitting, passion is that little pilot light that won't go out and keeps reminding you what you love, and encourages you to try again tomorrow.

What is passion to you? I invite you to take a Saturday morning at a coffee shop or your favorite quiet spot and spend a few hours pondering the question. You wouldn't be reading this book if you didn't want even more excitement in your life. Passion is a special gift. It needs to be appreciated and used well. Are you honoring yours as much as you could? Are others benefiting from your passion?

Lesson 2
Living a Passionate Life!

People are most familiar with situational passion, where a person is really passionate in one or two areas of their life. It may be a hobby or work they do, however, people who know them outside of that area wouldn't have a clue that they are a passionate person. For whatever reason, they don't use those same skills or excited attitude outside of that area. This type of passion is fine, but it's one or two-dimensional at best. I want a ten-dimensional life. I know it's possible, because I can see other people already live this way and I have myself, to a large extent.

Passion, as I am describing it in this book, is an

attitude, a way of living, and a way of being in the world.

I think it's pretty easy to spot passionate people. They tend to stand out in a crowd, even if they don't mean to. They seem to have an inspiring mentality about life, whether they are on the top of their game at work or shoveling with their kids. They have this certain energy about them even when they are sitting alone. It makes you wonder, *what's making them so happy?* Put them in the middle of a serious problem and they won't be sitting still for long. They are the people that get right to work, even if they aren't the strongest or the brightest. They would rather take charge and solve the problem, in order to do what they really want to be doing with their lives.

You won't find them in the typical time-waster activities very often. Arguing, conflict, and holding grudges are things they try hard not to get involved in because they know they are pointless. They would rather spend that same time enjoying or investing in life. They choose to minimize time and energy wasters. They want more from their experience of life, because passionate people have figured out one very important thing.

Do you know what people want more than time, money, or possessions? People want to passionately experience life. They want dynamic connections – where all of their senses are actively engaged by themselves and with others. That is a coveted wish above all else for the majority of people, if they dare admit it to themselves or others.

Author Joseph Campbell said it like this: "It's not like we are seeking the meaning of life anymore, we are seeking the experience of fully being alive."

Lesson 2 – Living a Passionate Life!

I call what Joseph is describing "dynamic connection."

Some people have figured out how to have a dynamic connection with a relationship, their art, or a cause. Others have never had that intense feeling. What I know for sure is once you have felt it, you want more. The way each person feels a dynamic connection may be different. It also doesn't mean it is all positive. Anger is a dynamic connection. It ignites all your senses to the point that you can hardly sit still. You can feel the physical reaction in your body as you pace or stomp your foot to defuse the energy. People don't want to be angry, but you can easily see the emotion of this dynamic connection throughout your body and mind.

Dynamic connections for you will depend on what type of a person you are. Talkers who are intellectual or emotional create deep stimulating conversation that gets them thinking and discovering new ideas. You can have a dynamic connection by yourself when you are engaged in something that gets you so intrigued that you lose track of time or forget to eat. Others may not want such high-level thinking. They prefer a more visceral fight, as in fight or flight, of competition. And, of course, there are people in between or all over the board as to what constitutes a passion for them. People may be shy to admit it but they lust for dynamic connections.

Look around, and you will see people living this way. They don't have a comfortable, checking-days-off-the-calendar kind of life. Their lives look more like getting-the-most-out-of-every-day-and-every-experience kind of life. They go for it! Trying things they have never done before, and saying "yes" to the fun stuff at least twice. They are intriguing people who you want to know more about. *How did they get this way? Was it hard? Did their irresponsibility or super accountability make this possible? Could I do the same thing?*

Essentially, Living a Passionate Life! is living life on your own terms in your words, thoughts and actions. It is not a simple task, but an incredibly rewarding one.

It's the question at the end of your life – *Did you really LIVE?* Or did you just exist and endure? When you are standing on the ragged edge of your existence, in that pivotal moment, right before you enter Heaven's gate, how will you answer?

I want to be able to say, "I gave everything I had every day, soaked up every opportunity, shared intimately everything I learned and did my best to inspire others to be their best selves and live their ideal lives. I don't have one ounce of energy left in me and I'm ready to surrender, satisfied in my purpose here."

What I'm talking about is not situational passion, but rather being passionate as a person in your entire life. It's a choice to connect to your essence and evolve above the typical issues of the world, and requires more of yourself and your contribution to life. It's an appreciation and wonder of all things; it's an eagerness to get the most out of every day. To intimately connect with every human being you meet as your teacher for something you need to learn.

Five things changed me from a person with situational passion to a person with attitudinal passion. They were:

First, **Life is too important.** I don't believe in the general attitude that "Life is too short." Andre has a grandmother in her 99th year who would tell you sometimes life is too long. She has had a wonderful life, but her body is not enduring as well as her mind,

Lesson 2 – *Living a Passionate Life!*

which is to be expected at her age. At times life is too short, like when my cousin died of cancer at 11 years of age. But I believe the real lesson is "Life is too important." All of our actions, inactions, thoughts, gestures, and decisions matter. There is not a day you aren't a role model for someone. How you decide to use your resources today will matter tomorrow. Carelessness causes harm. The lessons we are to learn here are pivotal to our lives and the fulfillment we receive. It is important to love fully with an open heart or you will have cheated yourself life's treasures. Because life is important we must put everything we have into it.

What you learn on your journey can help someone else learn that same lesson quicker, if you are willing to share. My poor children get "lessons" from me every day because I understand what I have already learned is so important in helping them prevent the same "school of hard knocks" lessons. That's the same reason I write Sofia Michaels books. I take a cathartic journey to make art of what I have learned so that it might help others.

Second, **I don't want to die with a half-used life.** In order to approach life attitudinally, you can't be afraid of it. To be afraid of life is to only half-live, cautious at every turn or decision. To approach every area of your life with courage would result in a much different experience. It would leave you breathless, scare the crap out of you, elate you, surprise you, confuse you, frustrate you, energize you, calm you, heap you with pain, entertain you, and please you. Life is Ying and Yang, up and down, polar opposites, messy and beautiful. It's by design that life doesn't come to you organized with a chronological flow chart. The bliss is in discovering and unfolding your own learning experience, and you can only get the full experience when you are not afraid to dive in deep and do it all.

Along with fully experiencing life is fully using your talents to make a difference in the world. A standard becomes, "did I give everything I could of myself today, or did I only give a portion of my potential?" It's easy to be lazy on a day you just don't feel like giving 110%. To feel like you have REALLY lived and left a legacy, you have to attempt it daily. This expectation is not about constantly "doing," it is also – and maybe more importantly – about being the best person you can be every day. That means when people are watching and when they are not. It means at the grocery store and at work. Ultimately, you do this for yourself because you understand the impact of living this way can have on everyone you encounter.

Third, **Life is what you make it**. I decided what kind of life I wanted to have and went after it, with intensity, until I got it. Any of my trying times, I saw as lessons I needed to learn. I chose not to stay where I was and blame it on unfair circumstances. I realized I could change it. In the end, I learned to play the hand I was dealt very well. Little did I know, my life would be great writing material, or something that "want-to-be authors" from an eventless life would give anything to have so they could write about it. My greatest excitement about this concept is understanding what a gift life is. The profound quote "you are a once-in-history event" motivates me to use my gift fully.

Fourth, **Make it a Great Day!** The power of one day is amazing over a lifetime. Once I realized the impact of one day, it changed my life. This concept represents two things: 1) It is my responsibility, and within my

Lesson 2 – Living a Passionate Life!

power, to make it a great day and 2) Carpe diem is achieved one day at a time. It means my day starts at 5 a.m. every day, whether I feel like it or not, because my body knows that is my power hour before my family gets up and the house gets busy. In this sacred time I read, write in my journal, work on goal setting, or just sit with a cup of coffee and reflect for a few minutes. It is by far the most impactful hour of my day when it comes to intuition and ideas.

This concept reminds me to be intensely present at every moment to fully experience my life. At times it's wonderful, and other times it's frustrating or scary. When my mind wanders and tries to worry about the future, I have to remind myself, *now is all there is.* Any of you who practice mindfulness know what I'm talking about. However, when you are fully present you notice that first bloom in spring, the mail truck pulling up to your mailbox, or a twinkle in your child's eye when she sees something that excites her.

When I was 25 I gave up that rotten game of *"you think your day was bad, listen to what happened to me."* It's toxic, and comes from a victim mentality. And who in their right mind wants to be the winner of that game? Instead, I got into the book *Feel the Fear and Do It Anyway* and changed my life. Everything I had every wanted in my life started to happen once I was proactive about it.

In 365 days of laser focus, I was able to make the biggest change in one category of my life. I thought would take ten years. It all started from a 100-day goal program and a sentence in one of its products that stated, "You can achieve in one year what previously took you ten." When I challenged that hypothesis, it worked! I haven't looked at the value of one day the same ever since that achievement. That's an intense attitude, and perhaps you don't want to go to that extreme – you don't have to. I wouldn't want to or be able to keep that pace constantly. After that, I allowed myself to meander and enjoy myself for three months. The whole experience was awesome.

Fifth, **Purpose and passion are connected.** This became the fuel that intensified the way I live. Once I discovered exactly what I am here to do and why, I became very focused on delivering my purpose. The blessing is how much joy and fulfillment comes from that. This is where you pay the price to go after your dreams. The joy doesn't all come at the finish line. It is in each sweet moment when you are living your bliss, feeling fully alive doing what you were meant to do, and being yourself, at its greatest intensity, that passion delivers. Once you have tasted that experience, it's almost impossible to go back to a mediocre way of living.

Yes, I am a type-A personality and my poor husband has loved and hated all that comes with a type-A personality driven on a mission. He knows I don't sit still very well. I am constantly thinking about how I can get our family to our goals. I exhaust him sometimes and he does the same thing to me, but in the end, we have been a great team with one purpose: our family. I need a purpose and a few challenges to feel totally alive.

People are suffocating in the rat race of life. The constant, chronic, multi-tasking priorities, until-you-flop-yourself-in-bed-at-night-exhausted-type-of-doing. They don't want their lives to be a blur of insignificant blah, blah, blah where they can't even remember what month it is, let alone day of the week. That's not a life, it's a treadmill. The problem is not working for corporate America or having a busy life. The problem is having an aimless life that is hectic.

What I have discovered is that the spirit of a human being needs two things – hope and purpose. Without hope our spirit dies, and without purpose we have no dynamic connection in the world. Without these two critical essentials, people are just surviving rather than thriving. We are not here to merely survive. With hope and purpose, people go on to thrive in amazing ways that benefit many other people in the world.

You can see that some pivotal life lessons changed my mindset from situational to attitudinal passion. Ever since I have embraced who I am and how important this experience of life is, it has been amazing. It's opened my eyes to what life can really be if you are open to its invitation – surrendering and trusting that whatever does happen is meant for your good. Living with attitudinal passion makes each encounter that much richer, each experience that much deeper and the feeling of fulfillment even better.

If you are familiar with Rick Warren's book *The Purpose Driven Life* he believes there are three levels of life – 1) Survival, 2) Success and 3) Significant. The survival level is when you are barely making it financially and feel like you are just checking days off the calendar. The success level is when you have a roof over your head and are living a comfortable life. The significance level is when "you are looking good, feeling good and have the goods (material possessions)" and you are living a purpose driven life.

Pastor Warren believes that you may systematically go from one level to the next, or you could be elevated from survival to significance, or fall from significance to survival and back to significance. According to him, the majority of people on earth are living at the survival level, which is incredibly sad. That means the majority of people are only barely existing, and not experiencing joy or contributing to others. If people are able to get out of the survival mode, they usually only go to the success level and would again have to work to get to the significance level.

While I understand his main premise of the levels, I disagree for one reason. His system says you can't have any significance (living your life on purpose, giving back, and making a difference) at the survival or success level. You can't tell me people don't contribute at those levels. I understand their main concern might be surviving. But anyone one, on any level, can contribute to society. Someone in prison (survival level) might be living their life on purpose by trying to inspire other prisoners not to offend again. A grandmother who's barely making it financially might be the soft place to fall for children whose parents are in chaos. She is certainly making a significant contribution to those children's lives.

If we were to tell all of the people perceived to be at level one or two that they don't really matter until they achieve significance, what a buzz kill that would be! We would have one apathetic country. Plus, everyone on the survival level would just be a drain on society and have no motivation not to be. I have spent more of my life at the survival level than not. Try to tell students I talked out of suicide, or their parent, that I had no significance in their lives. I may not have seen them after graduation, but I know I helped them get back in the game of life. I have had and seen countless examples of people at the first two levels being remarkable as human beings that I can't buy into his idea that significance only happens at level three.

My point in bringing this up is that you can live a passionate life no matter what level you are on. That includes having a strong purpose. You have to have a strong purpose to get out of survival mode. It was when I thought it was impossible or I was apathetic that I lingered there. It is easier to live a passionate life if you are living comfortably, of course. But it is often a taste of passion that ignites a fire which opens up a whole new world in which your life becomes better. Plus if you are never going to get to level three before you die, would you at least like to taste a passion for life?

There is not one person, regardless of circumstances, who couldn't choose to live a passionate life. Before you react, did you see I said choose? It is absolutely a choice people make every day. A large number of people don't choose to because they let the low-level distractions run their life. If you're guilty of that, just start with one hour focusing on Living a Passionate Life! Then increase it to one day, and finally increase it to every day as a habit or more importantly, how you live your life. You may run into trouble and have to start over. No problem, the important part is that you start over. Just think about how life would change if more people would say **yes** to Living a Passionate Life!

As this idea of Living a Passionate Life! started to evolve for me, I naturally began looking at what the concepts and components of it would be. The concepts would be the same for everyone, as they are the main foundation of the idea, but the way you go about each component of Living a Passionate Life! may be different based on personal style and preferences. By understanding the concepts and components you can at least see what makes up a passionate life if you prefer logical, concrete examples.

Concepts of Living a Passionate Life! are as follows:

Accountability – The experience you have with your life is ultimately up to you. There is no more blaming your parents, circumstances, or other people. Everyone has things happen in life. The people who are wasting their life blaming everyone but themselves are not Living a Passionate Life! On the other hand, people who understand "The life I want is up to me" are so much further on the journey than those who are crying, "life is not fair" and spewing excuses about why they can't have the life they want.

They understand they will have to own it when they win, but also own the results when they lose. Calculated risks are the same way. There are less days and years wasted because they know they have a limited time to be, do and have their ideal life. A large part of being accountable is setting goals, measuring your results, and determining what you can do better next time. A mature skill of being accountable is being able to give a sincere apology when it's needed.

One of the best motivators of being accountable is when you are unhappy or not satisfied. That feeling becomes the fuel that helps to propel you to change your situation. Negative and positive situations can be used as fuel for a person with high accountability. Accountable people, instinctively, want more of the positive and less of the negative. They also feel empowered to make that happen.

But perhaps the most amazing attitude they possess is "never quit." When things aren't easy, it is easy to quit. Roadblocks, mistakes, major change in plans, don't detour them. The mission is UNTIL you achieve the effect you want. Ordinary people do extraordinary things every day. So if you want to live a passionate life, you will keep at it until you get it. In the beginning, maybe you have a couple passions while you work on getting an attitude of being passionate about life. Or maybe, for the most part you feel you are Living a Passionate Life!, but one or two problems need your attention. Or perhaps you already are Living a Passionate Life! and you feel excited to raise the bar on that. Accountability will make each of those things happen.

Living on your own terms – People who live extraordinary lives tend to be non-conformist – not the going-to-jail kind of non-conformists, but the no-longer-tolerating-mediocrity kind. Mediocrity means no more than average. Non-conformists want to live an extraordinary life, regardless of their circumstances or financial ability. They don't use "can't" or excuses to keep them stuck in "good enough." They decide how they want to live, without being limited by what everyone else is doing, and figure out a way to make that happen. Throughout history we have always seen a few people who live and behave as a non-conformist. An example would be the frugal movement in the 1960s, where people refused to have a mortgage and instead found a way to buy land and live on it in makeshift quarters while they built a home as they could afford material. Today, there are non-conformists who have sold pretty much everything they own and travel the world doing work remotely wherever they are, because experiencing life is more important to them.

Non-conformity doesn't have to be that intense. It can simply be not willing to accept what most people do in favor of "there has to be a better way." While the majority of college students are saying it takes five years to graduate, I didn't have the luxury of taking five years because I didn't have the money. I had to graduate in four years so I could start working professionally. That meant taking as many credits over 12 as I could handle every semester because they were free. It meant going to summer school with more than a full load. I did graduate in four years. It wasn't easy, and often being a non-conformist isn't easy, but it was rewarding that fifth year when I was working.

Non-conformity might mean the dad stays home with young kids and the mom goes to work. For me, it means I have a wonderful relationship with my teenagers and love spending time with them. As a former high school teacher, I know teenagers can be wonderful people and I wasn't willing to accept the warning so many gave when I'd say I love my children – "wait until they are teenagers." Life doesn't have to be the way the majority of people live it. It can be the way you want to live it, if you ignore mediocrity.

Maybe ignoring mediocrity for you is being organic or vegan, perhaps refusing to have debt or not owning a car. Regardless of what your non-conformity is, there is one thing that rings true for all non-conformists. They care deeply, passionately about the thing or things they are non-conformists about. They are willing to sacrifice, be uncomfortable, be patient, stay committed, promote it to others, do it anyway if others won't join them, and in general make the non-conformity who they are even before it pays off for them.

Being a non-conformist offers real freedom from what everyone else is doing. When you feel no obligation to have to do as others are doing to be accepted, it really is your life you are living. You don't need validation, because what you are doing works for you and you're happy with it.

Living fully expressed – To live with a passionate attitude, you have to let your light shine. People who are living passionately are not worried about what other people think of them. They are not externally focused on what they should or should not be doing. They are focused internally on fully expressing who they are in order to make a difference in the world. There were people in my life who are not comfortable with me being a cathartic, self-expressed author. That didn't stop me from doing what I felt internally pulled to do. In the beginning it was not easy, as I broke my need to please people. But years later, I have come to understand that I have a responsibility to honor my life and calling. Diminishing myself in order to make other people more comfortable prevents my ability to help even more people. Part of my legacy is writing down or recording the life lessons I have learned so they may prevent others having to work so hard to get the lessons.

When we are being our authentic selves, we bring variety and interest to the world. That doesn't mean it's easy to accept everyone in their idiosyncrasies and values. But it makes it clear to see who we resonate with and who we don't. I can tell you quickly who I like and who I would rather not spend much time with. However, even the ones who cause you to have a visceral reaction of oil and water can teach you life lessons if you're open to it. When you have an intense reaction to someone – that's a hot spot – it means there is something going on within you that this person brings out. It's up to you if you want to explore it. You may think life would be easier if everyone was like you.

The truth is, it would drive you crazy. We need variety and interest to bring out the best in ourselves. We may want to be more like the people we like, just as the ones we don't let us know what we don't want to be like. All human interaction is valuable. Our responsibility is to be ourselves with social intelligence.

Intrinsic motivation – What helps you stay passionate about Living a Passionate Life! as you pursue it? Your first reaction might be the passion itself. But even when we feel passionate about something, it can ebb and flow. One very useful secret is to understand what motivates you in the first place. Different things motivate different people, such as social connection, awards and accolades, security, influence, or personal growth. If you use the motivation style that gets you excited the most, it can help you stay on track with your goals.

My motivation styles have changed over time. In my 20s and early 30s, security as well as awards and accolades motivated me. So I put myself in situations where I had an opportunity to gain those. Today, personal growth and influence matter the most to me. Being offered a shiny trophy for top salesperson of the year wouldn't give me any motivation. But being able to do something that would make a difference in the lives of others would motivate me. When you know what your motivation style is, you can use it to your advantage. It also prevents you from wasting time struggling to find motivation in ways that can't give it to you.

Motivation style is a tool we can use when it's available to us, and when it's not, we have to find the motivation internally. Intrinsic motivation is always the best kind because you can control it and it's renewable. When you are intrinsically motivated, you don't care if other people are motivated or not because you are paying attention to what you can do. This kind of motivation is often referred to as "a fire in your belly," synonymous with ambition or craving, which produces energy and determination to go after what you want.

People are often surprised that I have self-published six books. That means deciding to do it in the first place, choosing a topic that interests me enough to want to do it, writing 70,000-80,000 words by a self-imposed deadline, working with editors, graphic designers and a print-on-demand company to make them. I have never started writing a book that I haven't finished. It doesn't feel like work to me. I enjoy coming up with the idea for each book and cover, and love to see the final product come to life in my hands. I like capturing what I've learned. I like reading more to learn and figure out some more. When you are intrinsically motivated, no one has to tell you to get things done.

Being intrinsically motivated doesn't mean you only do what you want to. It means you are self-directed enough to get the yucky stuff done so you can get back to what you love. Intrinsic motivation is an internal drive to do what you have to do so you can live how you want to live. I would dare to bet it's a small percentage of people who are intrinsically motivated, but those who are benefit tremendously from it.

I've written a chapter on each component so that you can understand them in intimate detail in order to determine how you would like to go about them. Rather than explain what they are in detail here, I will list them so you can see a concise snapshot. Then you can enjoy each chapter for understanding.

Living a Passionate Life!

Components of Living a Passionate Life!
- Don't hold back (**Living a Dirty Life!**)
- Profound life experience (**Living La Vida Loca!**)
- Get out there and live (**Experiencing Life!**)
- Carpe Diem every day (**Make it a Great Day!**)
- Do work you are passionate about (**Passion Workers!**)
- Live a legacy (**Parenting Legacy!**)
- Have fun (**Having Fun!**)
- Have almost heaven on earth (**Almost Heaven!**)

Now you have a brief understanding of the concept and components of Living a Passionate Life! You know all "success" is predicated on finding what you are passionate about, then relentlessly pursuing every possibility to achieve your dreams. It's time to get very specific about what that means for you.

When most people are asked about their dream or ideal life, they start with a long list of being a millionaire, living in a mansion, having servants, big toys and even bigger travel plans. They don't know many of those people are actually very lonely and unhappy. Having things rather than people and experiences quickly hits a point of diminishing returns. I've seen this firsthand, and also read a lot about it over the years. For the majority of people, this pursuit would be in vain.

For me personally, I had a major shift about five years ago to being over the material part of life – perhaps it's just age. Now I care more about the people and experiences of life than the stuff. When it comes right down to it, what I want in my life is very simple: a lifestyle that supports my family's dreams, a balance between living for today and for the future, healthy food, exercise and spiritual practice, and a life driven internally by my passions rather than externally by things I don't care about. These are not passions, but rather the foundation I built my passions on which produced a priceless life.

Imagination is one of the greatest gifts you were given. It's the domain that allows you to create your ideal life if you want to. Plenty of people get uncomfortable when they hear the word "imagination" or "creativity" because they don't think they are creative. The truth is, everyone has an imagination and is creative. All you have to do is relax and give your mind permission to imagine your life, however you want it to be. At first, don't put any restrictions on it. My favorite place to do that is on one of the leather chaises in our bedroom. It reminds me of sitting on the porch at The Homestead when we were on vacation. Sit or lie down anywhere that's comfortable for you. When we are relaxed and comfortable, our mind will let go and our imagination will come out to play.

With this exercise, you are imagining how you'd love your life to be. You will never have it if you don't even know what would define your ideal life. When I say ideal, I mean ideal for your life right now. I have heard several people who have a hard time with the word ideal, like my friend Cindy. We were at a conference in Orlando. When we went to lunch, she said she didn't like the word "ideal" because her children would soon be leaving home. That didn't feel ideal to her. When she imagined her ideal life, it would not be as empty nesters so she felt stuck being able to imagine. Perhaps a better way to think about it is, "What's your best life now?" I couldn't be writing very easily if my children were younger. It's become ideal because they are pretty self-sufficient, and I can bring my laptop and write anywhere.

Once you have a general idea of what your best life would be, you can use your left brain, the logical side, to determine what you have to do, make action plans and timelines to start moving in that direction or move yourself quicker to achieving it if you're almost there. (I made a commitment to write as a professional coach but refrain from a how-to for this book.)

I am pretty much there – to a life on my own terms that I love. It certainly didn't happen overnight, and I worked my tail off and moved mountains to get here. It was worth it. It has also been fun – fun doing what I enjoy and fun defying the odds. We all have to realize that once we get to our best life, we aren't guaranteed to keep it. Turns of events happen all the time, challenges come and go, blessings come back around. What I've learned to do is enjoy it while I have it without concern that later I might not have it anymore. More joy has come my way because I now understand that.

If you just want to take a purely fun one-line question to the ideal life question, here is one for you to ponder: "If you could decide your message in a fortune cookie, what would it read?"

- You will experience amazing adventures -
- Love, family, and friends give you incredible memories -
- You will live a legacy of solving world hunger –
- Abundance makes your life blissful –
- Joy shows up everywhere you go -

Hopefully, by now we know each other well enough for me to just flat out ask you to make a list of your

Lesson 2 – Living a Passionate Life!

passions. Some people feel so shy about telling anyone out loud what they are passionate about. It truly isn't provocative at all. As more people get into this LPL! it will become as comfortable as asking what your favorite subject in school is.

If you're questioning what the difference is between likes and passions, there is a simple distinction. Do you like it or do you LOVE it? Like is like, love is LOVE. Passions are love. Likes also change more often. Passions can change over time, but they are usually not something you are totally into one minute and could care less about the next.

Mine look like this:

1. Having a family and being a mother.
2. Inspiring people to live their best life and using my life to inspire others.
3. Being debt-free.
4. Living my life on my own terms.
5. Teaching by writing Sofia Michaels books in great locations.
6. Public speaking.
7. Reading personal development books.
8. Learning personal development.
9. Enjoying nature.
10. Being creative.

So go ahead, list ten of your absolute passions before you move on. There is only one rule, and that is to start each passion with a verb (this book is about living, after all.)

Being passionate about ten things all at the same time makes for an overscheduled life. When you can go through your list of passions and narrow them down to five, you will have a much stronger view of what your core passions really are. Take the time to do the process of elimination and get your passion list down to your top five. Look at each passion you wrote, and decide "Can I live without this one?" It's like that survival island exercise they always made us do in school. If only half of us can survive, who is it going to be? While you are doing that it might also be helpful to decide are there any you can eliminate because they are more broadly covered in another passion you listed or could they be combined. For example, reading and personal development are my passion, and what I read for the most part is personal development books. Even when I read a business book, I am reading it for personal development so I could combine them into one passion.

Sofia Michaels' Top Five Passions

1. Having a family; being a mother.
2. Living life on my own terms.
3. Learning personal development.
4. Teaching by writing Sofia Michaels books.
5. Inspiring people to live their best life.

When you get all the way down to it, it is really as simple as having five main passions that drive your life.

Once you have your five defining passions, they become your guide more than your road map. The road to achieve them won't always be logical and methodical. It will be a combination of right-brained and left-brained thinking, and doing as well as a lot of just letting yourself be how you want to be. At first it may seem awkward, as you want a more definitive plan. But eventually you will get the hang of when you need to push, when to relax, and when to take a U-turn. You see, there is not one plan for everyone's life. Out of respect for the fact that we each receive the gift of one life, we must we take our own journey.

Again, remember your top five passions are not written as goals. They are used to define what your passions are in a concise manner. You could take each passion and turn them into goals or multiple goals for each passion. Then create an action plan for each goal, which could be used as a road map for your passions.

The reason it is important to define your passions is to help you clarify them. To help you focus on them. And then allow your conscious and unconscious mind to work on them. Our minds are constantly working, so to give it a goal or problem to solve, like "how can I live a more passionate life," our minds will work on it even if we've forgotten the question. If you write that question on a notecard and put it in your pocket or place it next to your bed, your mind will work on the answer for hours.

As we go forward in this book, we are going to explore each of the components of Living a Passionate Life! so that you can use them with your top five passions to create your own passionate life.

There are two reasons this book is so important and valuable. The first reason, and the problem, is the high percentage of people who are not satisfied with their lives. Numerous studies and surveys have been done in all categories of life revealing this, such as the survey by the American Psychological Association that found nearly half of all workers in the U.S. don't feel valued or adequately compensated in their jobs. Six in ten complain they don't have good opportunities for advancement. Or, a more interesting trend came from a Money Magazine survey that reported only one in four

Money readers said their top career priority was to land a promotion or raise; nearly half wanted more flexibility or more meaning in their lives.

The second reason is what the Money Magazine pointed to – the strong movement towards meaning or making a difference with your life that so many people are feeling right now. From the beginning of history, there have always been people who were more interested in their life having meaning than just worrying about themselves in a "survival of the fittest" mentality, thank goodness. But, there is definitely an emerging trend from conscious capitalism, The Bill and Melinda Gates Foundation, green education, and spirituality to volunteerism that allows you to see this trend.

Why this book is valuable is that it can show you the solution to these two problems even if you are already pretty satisfied with your life. The most exciting part of these two problems, or any other reason you aren't as satisfied as you could be with your life, is that you are completely in control of changing that. The difference between people who are Living a Passionate Life! and those who aren't is whether you accept a less than fulfilling life.

If you want to feel more alive and fulfilled in your life, keep reading.

As human beings, we tend to make things more difficult than they have to be. I certainly have been guilty of that by thinking *I just have to read one more book or re-try it this way that hasn't been working before I can actually figure it out.* Yet in this year when I came to the end of this project of deeply investigating passion and life, I discovered that both are simple when you get right down to them. Life is busy, hectic and overscheduled when we give too much interest in living externally by what others expect us to do, and we may not even want, rather than living by your values, priorities and passion.

To say *yes* to Living a Passionate Life! just turn the page.

Lesson 3
Living a Dirty Life!

If you are going to get the most out of life, you are going to get dirty. It's not possible to sit on the couch, calm, clean and cautious, to get a full sensory experience of all of the sights, sounds, tastes, and feelings life has to offer. No one gets through life unscathed. You are going to have dark times, heartbreak, sickness, and failures along the road of life. But the reason you are willing to get in there and really get dirty is because the reward when you fully experience life is so worth it that you are willing to do it all over again tomorrow.

Lesson 3 – Living a Dirty Life!

Life is not a journey to the grave
With the intention of
Arriving safely in a pretty
And well preserved body,
But rather to skid in broadside,
Thoroughly used up,
Totally worn out,
And loudly proclaiming,
WOW!!!! What a ride!
— Author Unknown

When I was a child, I spent one week a summer at YMCA camp. I had gone for several years before I was old enough to move up to "teen lodge." Teen lodge was the coolest because you were allowed more freedom, cooked your own dinners, got to shave your legs in the lake and didn't have to go down to main camp with all the younger campers. Legend had it that the coolest part of teen lodge was the mud hike. It was literally a mile or more of hiking in mud up to your waist or higher. Every camper attempting it had to bring special clothes for it that could just be thrown out when you were done, because they were never coming clean again. It was also a physical challenge, because the mud was heavy and unforgiving if you didn't have the strength to keep propelling yourself forward.

The day of our hike it was close to 100 degrees, and flies swarmed around every sweaty dripping part of you just to annoy you to the point of losing your temper. The beginning of the hike was not bad. It was actually a trough cut in the land to keep the mud in a relatively straight line along a trail. The first step was wet and cool, and perhaps more water than mud, so it was easy to move forward. I kept thinking, "This is so cool. Parents would never let us do this!" As we walked in a double-file line, the mud kept getting thicker and thicker. Clothes were "lost" along the way as the mud thickened and grabbed on in a greedy fashion to retain the tennis shoe that had come lose or the straw hat when a camper fell. The mud above the pit would dry hard as a rock on your hair, face, neck and shoulders. As the mud dried, it felt like your skin shrunk a size or two as one more annoyance you had to contend with.

When the wimps or babies had had enough they quit, crawled out of the mud trail, and walked back to camp as the mud quickly dried all over them in the blazing heat. The warriors of the group soldiered on to the end at all costs. As we were just about at the end, the pit got as deep as our shoulders for the short campers, like me, making it almost impossible to move. Just when you thought you were going to break out in tears and quit, the depth of the mud subsided. After we were victorious, we hooted and hollered all the way back to camp where we recounted each great feat and crazy incident.

How many people have gotten the chance to do that? How many people would take the chance if it presented itself? As a teenager, it just seemed an outrageous way to have "good clean fun." A shower could quickly fix everything. There was something about the fact that camp adults were allowing and encouraging us to do the mud hike that changed the way I looked at mistakes or messing up my life. It really wasn't such a big deal. You could almost always get out of it as we had proven on the mud hike.

When I was in elementary school I remember my mom letting my sister Diana and I play out in the rain with two neighbor children, Sean and Jeff. We thought that was so amazing because other parents didn't let their children do it. It was fun out in the cold rain. We ran all over the neighborhood without shoes and even laid down in low spots on the grass where the rain would pool enough to run over our bodies. I wondered why more people didn't have fun in the rain. Actually, I wondered why grown-ups acted like they were going to melt if they got wet running from their car to a building.

Over the years I had forgotten about the rain until one day. My daughter Mia had spontaneously invited her little sister Lexi to play out in the rain. They laughed and ran around our yard with lacrosse sticks, balls and buckets. When they finally came soaking wet to the front porch for a break, I had to run and get my camera to save the precious memory. Of course, it reminded me of the fun times I had in the rain with my sister, and gave me a big smile on my heart because my girls were having the chance to do the same.

A few more years went by. I had been on a seven-month streak of walking at least five days a week on a five-mile route in my neighborhood in the Town of Middleton. One of my neighbors, who was also a writing friend, would join me every once in a while. I walked in freezing weather and 100 degree weather. Part of the challenge was actually the elements I had to contend with in addition to the walking endurance. Often, I would try to dodge the weather by walking early or late. Then, there was the day a rainstorm was predicted, and the sky was already looking like deep black coal with wisps of thin white clouds. My neighbor offered to let me wimp out just when I remembered the mud hike and playing in the rain. I was determined. "Nope. We're going!" I proclaimed. The minute we took off it started pouring. The rain was coming down so hard it was difficult to hear each other as it poured over our mouths and ran down our clothing. Several times my friend offered to turn back, but at that point, we were already drenched. By the time we got back, I had to snap a picture in case I wanted to use it for this chapter.

As I looked at this picture I thought, *What grown woman and mom does this?* As I thought about it the same answer came back that always comes back – "I do." It made me laugh. It isn't that I'm an extreme adventurer or living a life that is so non-conformist that I shock all my neighbors. It is just that I have always been willing to do whatever it takes to get in there and get dirty in order to fully experience life.

Right now is all we've got. There is no guarantee of tomorrow. So while with your health and finances you can't have the attitude of living for today, in pretty much every other area of your life you can. While you are most likely familiar with *carpe diem (seize the day)*, I mean seize **your life**. A lifetime is an amazing gift and if you would seize it every day, every year, every decade just imagine the extraordinary experience you could have.

Do you realize life was supposed to be this way? – An experience where you are fully engaged and experiencing joy. Life was not meant to be a prison sentence where you have a flat experience, hardly seeing or feeling anything besides drudgery. Haven't you ever wondered why you were given the five (or six) senses? Each one of those senses was meant to give you pleasure interacting with people and your surroundings. I realize the senses are also used to protect us, but they could have been given to us with the purpose of pleasure. Someone thought to add joy to our senses on purpose. Perhaps it was so that we could embrace joy.

Here's a simple way for me to explain the two approaches – flat one-dimensional or full sensory. A flat, one-dimensional experience would be eating a meal by shoveling the food in one bite after another while you watch television. When you are done, your partner asks, "How did you like the smell of the cilantro?" You snap out of your daze and wonder, *What cilantro?*, as you don't even know what it looks like, smells like or tastes like. The experiential approach would be aware of the people who are eating with you, why they are important to you and what you enjoy about them. You would smell the sharp aroma of chipotle as you see the rich browns, oranges and yellows of the pulled pork as the sauce drips gently on your plate as you raise it to your mouth for the first bite that you won't soon forget.

Taking your time, hurrying up, relaxing, tensing up – all effect your experience in the moment. Can you hear the first bird of spring gently chirping outside your bedroom window? Did you notice the first bud of a spring flower? Can you tell by the sound of a voice who is on the other end of the phone? What would make your eyes tear up from beauty? When was the last time you saw your romantic interest and they made your heart race with excitement? Is your life as exciting as you'd like it to be?

If you want to live an engaging life, there is one very important commitment you'll have to make. **Be open.** Open to whatever may come your way in a day – open and non-judgmental. Open to signs of grace. Open to three very important aspects

1) People
2) Experiences and
3) Opportunities.

Be open to people. Sadly, we are conditioned to only be kind, inviting and supportive to certain people who meet the rules and conditions we have set for our lives. You certainly did this in high school if you conformed to the clique as you were assigned, and continued this type of barrier behavior where certain people got access to you and others didn't. Don't feel too bad, because people did this to you as well. Typically, we have this society that doesn't have an approach to people where we find it rich to have a wide variety of people with all colors, ages, backgrounds and lifestyles in our personal repertoire. We often play it safe by just befriending people like ourselves. From a business, socio-economic or political view that might make sense, as experts say we have the same economic value as our five closest friends. Yet from a pure relationship viewpoint, we miss so much when we are so narrowly focused.

The truth is every person who crosses your path in life has something to teach you, if you are open to it. Even that totally crappy boss, who you can hardly stand to deal with each day, is perhaps reminding you that you need to stand up for yourself and make a firm decision about what you are no longer willing to tolerate. That little neighbor kid who you can hear laughing in his backyard might be reminding you to lighten up and have some fun. And that 90-year-old widow might suggest you be kinder to your spouse, because it's a long road to be alone for 40 years. If you can open your heart each time you encounter someone, you never know what that person could add to your life.

Some people will be a brief encounter, others may stay for a season and some may be with you for years. We aren't used to that dirty approach to ending relationships, either, because we are taught to feel bad when relationships, employment and the like come to an end. We are "supposed to" keep it clean and maintain the relationships at all costs, unless we have a very valid reason that society would give us the stamp of approval to leave. It's still a dirty exit, but a socially approved one which may sit better with you then the fact that the season on that relationship simply came to an end – you don't meet each other's needs anymore.

One thing that helps a dirty end to relationships, employment, etc. is to think of them all as assignments in life school. Each one you sign up for is an assignment to teach you life lessons. We understand that each school year ends when we have learned the lessons well enough to progress to the next grade. Can you imagine telling anyone it's "not nice" to leave second grade? We actually do the opposite – we celebrate when someone moves on to the next grade or "graduates" a certain level. We don't think second grade or the second grade teacher is horrible. We simply understand it was time to move on.

People teach us all kinds of lessons, from good to bad to ugly. They are all important and necessary to our experience here. If I want to learn something that is beyond where I currently am, a mentor can be incredibly valuable when it comes to stretching me much further and faster than I could on my own. How do I learn the type of people I don't want in my life? – By encountering them. This attitude that you can learn something from every person who crosses your path, whether for a moment or a while, can add unbelievable depth to your life.

Be open to experiences. When we were little, we were open to all kinds of opportunities in big, small and interesting shades of excitement. It was easy to say yes because we had an attitude of "everything is play." Why wouldn't we say yes? At that time in life, we were interested in learning anything and everything we could get our hands on. If we didn't like something, it took us two seconds to toss it to the side and keep eating up the next sensation that came our way.

Life is interesting. There are so many languages, foods, places and styles to keep us entertained if we would approach life like a child who is eager to play. Just think about what you have never done before. Perhaps a sleigh ride, salsa dancing, mind orgasms, a silent retreat, speed dating, a Christmas without gifts, drive a Zamboni, give someone your paycheck, celebrate a failure, downsize, go electronic free for 24 hours, donate your organs, focus on gratitude for 30 days, sleep on a beach overnight, create a report card for yourself as a human being, decide if you even want a funeral, ...

Experiences are more than a bucket list. It's also the gifts of an ordinary day like a healthy check up, watching your children flourish, an unexpected kiss in the middle of the day, awesome sleep because your day was fulfilling, someone believing in your dreams, having your needs met, or evolving as a human being.

Experiences are a verb consisting of: observing, encountering or undergoing something personally. If you weren't there, you didn't experience it. Vicarious experiences are not real, they are entertainment. I might be able to learn something from it or experience a mild joy, but the intensity is nothing compared to a first-hand experience. Experiences have a way of changing you, if you allow it. Hence, we gain practical wisdom from observing, encountering or undergoing something. Living is a verb that is full of experiences.

As humans, we are creatures of habit. We tend to go to the same places, with the same people, on the same days of the week. Even if we have a major change to our lives of moving to another state, losing a job, or even winning the lottery, research on post-traumatic growth tells us we would be "used to" that new lifestyle habitually within three years. At that point, we would not go out of our way to have new or different experiences. Whether we are having big changes in our lives or not, there are two things that are critical to getting the most out of what we experience. The first is awareness of how important experiences are, and the second is a commitment to experiencing life.

In order to live a passionate life we have to be committed to experiences throughout our whole lives. We can never get too comfortable and give up the ING of life (living.) That doesn't mean we constantly have to be in motion, as relaxing, meditating, and sleeping are also part of ING. Work backwards. What do you want to experience this year, this quarter, this month, this week, this day? Can you make a commitment right now to get up every day and fully be open to experiencing life? When you can do that, your life will really change. By others seeing you live a passionate life, you may change their lives too.

Are you someone who says "yes" or "no?"

Be open to opportunities. When someone offers you an opportunity, get in the habit of saying yes even if it's out of your comfort zone. Opportunities are the gateways to who knows what could happen. That's what's exciting about them. What if something amazing could happen when you accept an opportunity? Not every opportunity turns out to be good, but are you playing life to win or are you playing not to lose? There is a big difference in those two distinctions. For a long time I played not to lose, without even realizing it. I was cautious. I was protective because I didn't want to lose what I had worked so hard to gain. I wasn't open to opportunities where I could have gained a lot more. The other "playing not to lose" thought is the idea that *I don't have much so I can't afford to lose it.* Some would argue that's exactly when to take an opportunity because you don't have much to lose.

Personal development experts will tell you that preparation, meeting a favorable time or occasion, is the meaning of a good opportunity. If you aren't educated on rental properties and a four-unit apartment complex is for sale at an excellent price, that opportunity may not go well if you can't be disciplined with the rental income to pay the mortgage, taxes and save for maintenance. You could end up having to sell the property or worse yet, lose it to foreclosure. After the fact you may realize what you did well, what didn't work and what you would do different next time. However, the opportunity would have been a ton better if you were prepared for what you were getting yourself into.

These wild, uneducated, throw-caution-to-the-wind-and-who-cares-if-you-get-hurt-kind-of-opportunities aren't the kind of opportunities we are looking for. Hearing about an opportunity like the four-plex might get you interested in learning about real estate investments, and the next time one comes up you may be ready to go after the opportunity. This is not to say we should say no to every opportunity we aren't 100% ready for, but you do need to use your common sense.

When preparation meets opportunities, amazing

things can happen. What can you do to make sure you are prepared for the opportunities you want to have in your life? I have five keynote speaking topics ready to present in case I meet someone who is looking for a speaker. My children do their homework and get good grades in case the opportunity for scholarships presents itself. I make sure I am showered and in a sharp outfit when I go to networking events because I never know who I will have the chance to meet. Being prepared also means getting out in the world and being in places and situations where opportunities can happen. There are not a lot of opportunities that will come to you sitting alone on your couch.

One thing that is very interesting is when you start looking for or paying attention to opportunities, they will show up often and in all kinds of sizes and shapes. Someone has tickets to a concert they can't use, would you like them? Mortgage rates dropped below 3%. An employment position you would like to advance to opens up. Someone is interested in being friends. You get asked on a date. A referral allows you to achieve a goal. Opportunities are everywhere if you look for them. People who are living a passionate life are open to opportunities at all times.

You will need to have one more thing that is very important in order to live a more passionate life, and that is an open heart. Have you ever thought about that before? Do you already have an open heart, or are you wondering what that even means? An open heart is a loving, compassionate heart that is able to both give and receive love. An open heart allows you to love yourself for all of the beautiful aspects of your spirit, and also embrace the mistakes and bad decisions you have made without deeming yourself a lost cause. With an open heart it is much easier to learn from your mistakes and move on, rather than remain in guilt and continually punish yourself for your transgressions.

An open heart attracts positive into your life. A closed heart turns to stone and leaves you feeling all alone. Where a closed heart repels people, an open heart invites people. The open heart looks forward to living each day. When we have an open heart, we can receive the joy and gifts in life. People with an open heart are evolved and see the bigger picture of why we are all here on earth. In order to believe whole heartedly in the idea of "Survival of the Fittest" you would have to close your heart to not notice who gets hurt and not care about them.

To have an open heart is an important life lesson, and perhaps a challenging thing to do at times because it can get messy. Have you dared to love and it ended in a broken heart? Perhaps you closed your heart a little or a lot for a while, or too long. Maybe you were even a sassy, angry heart for a few months while your disappointment and rejection mended a bit. Somehow dopamine helps open your heart again when you encounter a spirit who manages to send it soaring throughout your body. Our hearts are amazing.

As you know, your heart is not just for romantic relationships. My heart has always been open to babies, little children, and teenagers, but especially children who have not been dealt a good start in life. I feel like they need love and compassion the most. However, in recent years my open heart has learned that our elderly are often forgotten and tossed aside because we don't value them like other cultures do. They need as much love and compassion as little children. Children grow up and move on with their

Lesson 3 – Living a Dirty Life!

lives, and eventually the elderly die. Was it worth them being in your life? If you live with an open heart you would say "absolutely" and not want to hold them back because you are going to feel dirty pain when they leave you. Although life is dirty sometimes, it is all worth it in the end to live with an open heart. The joy, laughter and lessons you gain can be priceless.

Do you have an open heart at work? For some reason, work can be as catty as high school, with certain people not talking to certain people while elements of jealousy and sabotage lurk about, although no one would admit it. The work environments with closed hearts are dysfunctional at best. I'm not saying it is always easy to keep your heart open professionally, but I guarantee it increases productivity and satisfaction at work.

Start to pay attention throughout your day. Every once in a while, check "Is my heart open?" You will quickly be able to tell when your heart is open and immediately feel it when it closes. Here's an easy visual for you to see what it feels like when you close it. Let's say you are tired after work and stopped at the gas station to fill up your tank. The gas pump won't accept your loyalty card and final payment so you are slightly annoyed as you fight the wind to go inside to ask the cashier for help. As you approach the store, you see two disheveled people blocking the door. A third person has his hand on the handle holding the door open just a crack. There's no way you can avoid encountering these people and quickly get inside. What would be your first impulse when you come upon this scene? The vast majority of people would say "My heart immediately closed because I didn't want to deal with these people." If you agree, that is what it feels like when your heart closes. Knowing this sensation can help you be aware and choose to keep your heart open.

Choosing to keep your heart open benefits everyone. Most importantly, when you approach life with an open heart you make an impact on people's lives as well as your own. The gas station encounter could be very different if you approached it with a smile, looked each person in the eyes and said "How are you doing today?"

I wasn't born with a silver spoon in my mouth. I had the fortune of learning early that if I wanted something, I had to go get it myself. When most teenagers go after their first job, they are a little scared. Not me. I walked to Hardee's, the only minor age hiring business within walking distance of my home, clean showered and dressed up (way too dressed up for the job) and when the manager asked me the last question, "You don't have any experience. Why should I hire you?" Without pausing, I looked him straight in the eyes and firmly said, "Because I am going to be the best cashier you have ever had." He hired me, on the spot, and I was. For two years I was the customer favorite on drive-up and had a blast.

It's easy to understand that you have to be passionately aggressive to go after what you want in life, but there is an underlying dirty attitude that will make you even more successful. That attitude is "whatever it takes!" Plenty of people will say that, but only a few will actually do it. Traditional marriage vows say that, but what some divorcing couples really meant was "until it gets inconvenient." Whatever it takes means pulling more than your weight, even when others aren't. People with a "whatever it takes" attitude don't keep track of what's fair because they already know it's not fair. If they want something, they can't distract themselves with a pity party.

As I've said, I have always been this way. One day, Andre asked me to get under the van and apply a patch to the Y pipe, since he only had the van up on small ramps and couldn't fit under it. Even though I didn't know how, I didn't hesitate. I just got under the van. Andre had given me some gloves so I wouldn't burn my hands and safety glasses. He then crouched down to instruct me how to apply the patch. Once I understood what he wanted me to do he left and quickly came back with the camera. I sighed, "Oh, geez" and Andre responded, "I want a picture." Since I'm the one who is constantly taking or offering to take pictures (yes, my teenagers love me), it certainly wouldn't be fair to refuse him. So Andre took the picture – no big deal.

What became a big deal was the reaction from people when Andre posted it on Facebook. I didn't care and didn't think it was a big deal. People were appalled that Andre asked me to fix our van, and worse yet, took a picture of me in this horrendously "not wifely" activity. The photo ended up getting 34 comments, which tells you it got a reaction. First of all, they didn't know I was happy to do it. I am fiercely committed to not having a car loan, and I appreciated that Andre had figured out how to fix the problem. Second, the photo was a gesture to my biological dad who was an auto mechanic. But my husband captured it best when he posted "this picture sums up my beautiful wife of 16 years. (Always willing to do whatever it takes to get the job done) Love you honey!" He was right, the picture does sum up my "whatever it takes" attitude and I'm proud of that.

One thing needs clarifying though, "I'm willing to do whatever it takes as long as it's legal, ethical and not against my marriage vows." That is another one of my famous sayings.

Maybe you aren't willing to get under a car, refrain from dessert, or give up a kidney. But where are you willing to get a little dirty with a "whatever it takes" attitude in order to live a more passionate life? A few questions could help you answer that. What do you stand for? What are you fiercely committed to? What do you want to accomplish at all costs? What are you willing to do to be your best self? How will you live a legacy? When you are not satisfied, how will you change that?

We'll come back to these questions, but first I need to talk to you about two specifically dirty parts of life that are not as literal as some of the experiences we have been talking about so far. However, they are critical to Living a Passionate Life! As I have said, this entire chapter goes along with the fact that no one gets through life unscathed. That includes all of the categories of our lives. i.e. health, career, family/friends, financial, personal, spiritual, recreation, community. We may be great in one particular area our whole lives, like finances, yet in another area, like relationships, we keep failing miserably. Perhaps you have taken a digger in the ditch in all the categories of your life at times. Or maybe you've been "lucky" so far and just keep holding your breath that you won't break down. That's no way to live. I can't name one person who didn't get dirty while they were fully participating in life, and I bet you a million Twinkies you can't either.

The first dirty category is the relationship you have with yourself or personal development and the second dirty category is love. Ewww..., Did you have a negative reaction to that? See what I mean? These two areas can get to be a complete mess at times, but something about them keeps you coming back to try again, even when you swear you are done and never going to allow "them" to hurt you again? The reason is because personal development and love make you feel alive, and that feeling and those experiences are worth the dirt you may get into at times. I am sure you already get what I mean, but let me take you on a full sensory experience just so you get the full effect.

Personal development sounds so professional and impersonal, so I'll call it what it really is – the relationship you have with yourself. That's more intimate, isn't it? Do you like the relationship you have with yourself? Do you like yourself? Are you the best person you possibly can be at this age and stage of your life? Is your self-talk healthy? Or is that little voice in your head your worst critic? Do you feel confident and certain about who you really are at the core of yourself? What would you say are a few dirty little secrets about yourself you don't want people to know?

We can all make a list of the things we don't like about ourselves or the mistakes we keep making. Living a Dirty Life! would be the willingness to get in there and improve yourself to the point of being your best self. It would be the willingness to share with others where you need help or a resource. For myself, personal development is one of my top interests and why I write Sofia Michaels books. I read up to 22 hours a week, have attended over 400 seminars, etc. None of that means I think I have it all figured out. It means I'm really willing to get dirty trying to evolve and help others do the same. It certainly doesn't mean I have no problems. It means I'm willing to live the best I can in spite of them. Hence, getting dirty is part of the experience and development. Often it is our hardest to overcome lessons that make the greatest impact on who we become.

Take a look at your own life right now and some time to reflect. How have you developed as a person over time? It's worth a day of your life to examine that. Were you high-maintenance at one point and now you've learned to get your happiness, care and concern primarily from yourself? Were you part of the stuff-itis culture and now you're on track with your financial goals? Were you once a toxic person and now realize you want to put positive energy into the world? Have you gotten the drama out of your life? Have you re-wired all of your bad habits? Are you denying any part or trait of who you are? Are you going after what you want in life?

Part of getting dirty, so you can clean things up, is acknowledging where you are doing well, what needs to improve, and what you can do better next time. People who know me well realize I am very self-aware – that means the good and the bad of who I am, what I like and don't like, where I've been and where I'm going. Tools that help me do that are journaling, goal work, year-end reviews, discussions, etc. Most people don't want to put that kind of effort into personal development. What they are missing is the benefit of being able to look back over that work and see their progress. For example, since 2003 I've done a year-end review to capture my life lessons each year. The review included all of the categories of my life as well as my three biggest accomplishments, three biggest failures, how I've changed as a person and one final question – what I will do differently next year based on what I learned last year.

Lesson 3 – Living a Dirty Life!

I can look back to 2003, my first year as a full-time entrepreneur, and quickly flip through to the current year. In hindsight, I can see the real estate bubble and burst, the best decisions I made for my family, exactly when I learned to value myself, the brave things I've done, what I shouldn't have done, and the impact I made for others. That's a pretty cool snapshot of my life that goes deeper than pictures and mementos. For most people, their life is a blur. "I kind of remember that period of my life when I struggled with ..." "Did I used to enjoy ...I don't remember that very well." "Was that a "good" or a "bad" year? It was five years ago so I have no clue." The important point is not that you have to be a historian of your life. It is that there is so much value in learning from your life and you can't do that if you aren't examining it. Examining can be messy and also fun, intriguing, and very rewarding.

The opposite of a fully examined life is holding your breath to survive and being glad "that" (whatever that is) is over with. Do you want your life to be about holding your breath, or about being fully engaged? There were times in my life that I held my breath. It seemed all I could do to get through the tough times, but I have learned that the willingness to get in there and get dirty discovering what's really going on, so I could fix it, was much more beneficial in the end. Each time, I learned I am stronger than I thought I was. My worst fears never happened. It's satisfying to understand what's happening in my life.

By this stage in my life I understand and fully accept that everything that is happening contributes to who I become. Some things I may never understand, some I will understand while it's happening, and other things I will understand years after they have passed. Knowing that, and respecting it, makes it easier. I don't struggle to understand when it's too early for the meaning to be revealed to me. I am fully confident that the meaning will come to me if I am supposed to know it. That's another example of being willing to allow some dirt in your life, because in the end it will benefit you.

So this brings us to the second category of life that can get quite dirty at times and that is love, romantic love. We idealize this topic in order to entice people into it, especially if they have been brokenhearted in the past. It was actually very smart of God to create a naturally occurring chemical reaction called dopamine to entice us to a romantic partner. I'm certain that's one of God's little tricks. When people say, "I wasn't in my right mind. I was in love." That is actually a literal explanation of what happens. Dopamine is a feel-good reaction in our bodies that gets you to do all kinds of crazy things like move across the country to be with your loved one even though you have no job, get married within weeks of knowing each other, or give up your life as you know it to be with this person.

The beginning part of love is usually not messy. That's supposed to be the easy time when you compromise quickly, choose each other over others, and enjoy the best parts of having a partner. When the dopamine wears off, and long-term love begins, we tend to hit patches of dirt at times: like career choices, raising children, serious illness, financial challenges, or "growing apart."

I remember when this changed for me with Andre. From the moment we met we have always had a strong fiery attraction to each other. Yet by the time we had three children and had owned three homes, I noticed something different about my feelings for Andre. The difference actually made the dopamine phase seem frivolous and unimportant now. This new feeling was much deeper and didn't seem to care what he was wearing or if he had kissed me that day. It was an awe of the fact that he was the father of my children and committed to our family. It was an appreciation that he was a loyal man. It was gratitude that I was not alone in life. It was respect for the fact that he was not a quitter.

Being the creative, impulsive person I am, I blurted out in a pondering kind of voice, "I don't think I'm in love with you anymore," when I saw Andre shaving at the sink. He was a little surprised and quietly said "What do you mean?" I responded with, "It's something much bigger than that. I mean I really, really love you. When I think about everything we have been through together and everything you have given me, it just makes me cry." Andre knew how important our marriage, children and a home were to me, as I had wanted them my whole life.

"I guess I mean I love you. Not infatuation, but a real, deep and committed love and that is so much better," I finished. Andre's reaction was "Well, that's good. Me too." He understood what I was trying to say although I was not saying it well.

That kind of love is what is needed to make it through the days you don't even like each other. When others talk about how the "grass is greener," you know the grass is greener where you water it. It takes that kind of love to mean our marriage vows, "…, for better or for worse, for richer, for poorer, in sickness and in health, to love and to cherish; from this day forward until death do us part."

Those vows talk about the really good times and the

really dirty times over a lifetime. The people who tell you their marriage has been nothing but a wonderful romance are telling a story. I for one will tell the truth. Marriage is an incredibly challenging institution, especially when you enter it young and want to be in it until you die. How could you know when you pick your spouse at 24 what he will be like as a middle aged man? When you choose a single woman with no attachments, how could you know how much she'll change when she becomes a mother?

And yet when you are willing to get dirty in the harder parts of life you also gain a love like no other – someone to wake up next to, share the work with, confide in, and face the world twice as strong. That's what makes the challenges worth it. Andre use to get offended when I'd say "I'm a married personality." I think he took it to mean I'd be happy married to anyone, which is absolutely not the truth. It means the opposite of *I'm a single personality* – people who enjoy dating and the life that goes with it. I like being married with one man as my life partner where we have routines, foods, places we like to go that are comfortable and familiar. We have become like a cozy sweatshirt that is so familiar and re-assuring. Andre knows if I pat him on the behind in public, I'm nervous. Just as I know if he's acting up, it's Thursday night. That's the kind of comfort that comes with twenty years together, and I would choose that over the butterflies of first dates any day. There's enough spice for me in the dirt we get into now and then.

I remember Dr. Phil saying one time, "It takes two very mature, highly accountable people to be married" and he is right. When you are able to work to a place where you are two very mature, highly accountable people, life becomes easier and more rewarding. That is part of the reward for working through the not-so-great times. When we were married seventeen years, we both jokingly agreed we had the experience and skills to be married now.

The other thing that can happen when you leave the dopamine stage for true love is an understanding that the idea that you are half of a couple is incorrect. One whole person plus one whole person makes two people, not one. This may seem like semantics, but it is actually a very important concept. I can't be half of myself in order to be a couple with you. A mature person needs to be completely authentic regardless if they love someone or not. On the same line, I am not defined by my husband nor is he defined by me. We are two independent people who have chosen to legally, financially and intimately be together and raise children.

Perhaps the more challenging part of a couple, consisting of two whole people, is allowing your partner to BE – who they are. This would mean you take the focus off what you'd like to change about your partner and put in on yourself as a reminder to just let your partner BE. I'm not talking about being a doormat if they are breaking boundaries or not being a good partner. Rather the freedom of dancing, talking and being in the world the way he naturally is. You'll find when you can both do that the relationship is more enjoyable.

We have learned to allow each other to BE. Last spring Andre had a conference for work in Clearwater Beach, Florida and I went along. I'm happy to be venturing out to the beach and local venues to write part of this book while he does his work and we meet up at night to enjoy some time together. One of my favorite dates was at The Cheesecake Factory where Andre always orders a Windsor 7 and steak with baked potato and I have a margarita, shrimp Alfredo and turtle cheesecake. But what was even more fulfilling for me was our conversation about the question "What do you need to do to live a more passionate life?"

Andre isn't always open to discussions like that, but this night he was interested, engaged and even complimentary about what I had been doing with my life in the last couple years. He has no idea how attractive he is to me when he's like that. I won't disclose our conversation because it included intimate details about each of our passions and what we wanted to do with the rest of our lives. After so many years together, that's one of the ways we stay connected and try to support each others' dreams.

Andre and I are opposites who attracted – calm, logical and stable to chaotic, high-energy and strong-willed. For the last twelve years Andre has worked for a large corporation and I have been a full-time entrepreneur for a decade, after I was laid off from teaching. Over time we have mellowed and blended a bit, but remain strong opposites with common values. We have found a way to work together that we both benefit from. With our children we have common goals and two styles of achieving them so when one doesn't work the other can take over. Perhaps it is the idea that we are attracted to what we don't see in ourselves that works for us.

The truth is, the longer we are together the more painful it will be for one of us to lose the other one. We were at a hotel for a basketball tournament and Andre and I were sitting next to the pool when a couple in their 80s got into the pool together. They were so sweet to each other as they slowly moved around in the pool, constantly helping each other. Andre commented how neat that was and my reaction went from one of compassion to how hard it will be when one of them dies. I am rarely pessimistic. I realized this was my fear of happiness popping up again.

Would I really not want to have love for a lifetime if it was going to be painful when I had to let him go? Of course, I would choose love. In order to experience love, you have to be willing to get dirty sometimes and fully go for the love you want. Being cautious about love is like driving with one foot on the gas and another on the brake. While you could functionally do this, it will not give you the same fulfilling experience as driving a little faster than the speed limit and enjoying the ride with the windows down and the music cranked up on a gorgeous day in June.

What I respect the most about Andre and me is how committed we have been to our marriage vows. No matter how challenging (dirty) our lives have ever gotten, neither one of us ever quit. It would have been easy to quit many times. Each of us would have had reasons society would understand if we did. But personally, each of us would have felt like a quitter, which neither of us is. The truth is, every time we have held on and worked through whatever the issue was, we are so glad we never quit.

It's in the sweet, clean part of life that we have stability, an intact family, a partner, and have achieved a good number of our dreams. That is why, as a wife, I am willing to do whatever it takes, get as dirty as needed, and hold on until joy comes, because it always does.

By now I hope you feel differently about getting a little dirty in life where you are fully engaged and experiencing all life has to offer you, rather than sitting pretty and safe on the couch. No one keeps a clean track record their whole life. Just think of how many experiences, people and opportunities are given up when we think we aren't ready to jump in. Where in your life can you just jump in and figure it out later? What are you willing to do in the next three minutes to live a more passionate life? Get used to asking yourself that question, often.

If you embarrass yourself or mess up, who cares? We all need to be able to laugh at ourselves as human beings and be able to get up, without taking forever, to dust ourselves off and try again. As if we have never failed before. This chapter should also make you feel that mistakes, false starts and do-overs are not that big of a deal most of the time. It's more important that you went for it. Being willing and getting started are the two key ingredients people on the couch of life are missing. What are you willing to do to live a more passionate life? When are you willing to get started?

Remember earlier in this chapter where are you willing to get a little dirty with a "whatever it takes" attitude in order to live a more passionate life. A few questions could help you answer that. What do you stand for? What are you fiercely committed to? What do you want to accomplish at all costs? What are you willing to do to be your best self? How will you live a legacy? When you are not satisfied, how will you change that?

Lesson 4
Living La Vida Loca!

What if you had to stop at periodic times in your life and be evaluated on how you are handling your one shot at life? What if, depending on how well you were doing, your life was allowed to continue or be expired? What if there was no getting around this review process? Would you go about your life differently? Or would you give up and let your life expire?

How "well" you are doing wouldn't be reviewed with the traditional Western society scale of income, degrees, square footage, titles, vanity, vehicles, etc. It would be measured against;

- Are you seizing the profound opportunity your life

is?
- Are you living with meaning and purpose?
- Are you living your values on your own terms?
- Are you investing your life in something greater than yourself?

Would you be happy with how you are doing? Would you be willing to review these four questions in the morning before you start your day to set your intention for the day, and again at bedtime to review how you did? Give it a try. This simple habit could change your life.

Most people don't treat each day of their life like the extreme opportunity it is. We tend to have the idea that life is long, so we can take our time getting around to the things we really need or want to do. If you were given a 30-day notice that your turn at the game of life will expire, would you have a newfound urgency to intensely live? We get the importance or intensity when we pretend our life is literally on the line. This type of "30 days to live" exercise is fine for brainstorming a bucket list or goals. However, it is not realistic to think this motivation can be maintained or is even a healthy focus.

The primary problem with this approach is that it's not realistic. If I knew my days were really numbered, I would not work. I wouldn't even second-guess that or feel guilty about it. My life insurance would more than make up for that. The problem is, Andre can only get that money if I die, so realistically, I want to and have to work. If I knew I was going to die very soon, I wouldn't discipline my children or try to teach them anymore. I would love and enjoy them as much as I could, as that is what is appropriate given the

Lesson 4 – Living La Vida Loca!

situation. This approach to parenting wouldn't work in real life either.

So you get the point that we can't go all the way over to *The Holiday* (great Queen Latifah movie on this point) kind of living where we can quite easily live with a zest that is ten levels better than what we are doing right now. I believe it is absolutely a godsend that the majority of us don't know when we will die. Human instinct would have you living scared all the time. That is not a healthy way to motivate yourself.

Life is crazy, at least at this point in history. It's not the 1950s, where one car, a one-bathroom home and one salary took care of a whole family. Today it takes more than two full-time jobs to afford whatever crazy life we said yes to before we could afford it. Back then we didn't have as many divorced, blended families, or single parents. This dynamic creates layers of energy that we don't get to completely control. Today we have expanded and polluted to a scary level that may not allow us to sustain our planet. "Work-life balance" is not even possible for the majority. For the first time in history, children are not expected to outlive their parents due to obesity. And even if you say you're not into watching reality television, how much drama do you have in your own life?

Life is crazy. Not because of any of these things, but because of the profound – once in a lifetime – opportunity it is. You specifically were allowed to come here at this exact time in history with a certain number of days, a unique purpose, talents, and DNA. Then, each decision you make and don't make, along with each action you take or don't take, moves you along on the journey and impacts other people's lives. We don't get to go back and have a do-over. At each age and stage we are novices doing it for the first time. We all have to do the best we can with what we have and who we are at that precise time.

In hindsight, hopefully we are smarter, but you can only use that wisdom for reflection and doing better going forward. There is no future sight. We are each playing this game of life, for real and in real time, with no inside peek at the victorious playbook to guide us.

Plenty can distract us from the real purpose here in the life school. Many of them are things I just mentioned. Yet people *Living a Passionate Life!* aren't distracted. They are laser focused on what's important and avoid unnecessary distractions. To spend one hour talking about how so-and-so did this and that and the drama that creates for the family is not an option for them. They know exactly and quickly if they want to put time and energy into something. That's not rude, it's personal choice. Showing respect for the fact that each of us gets to decide exactly everything about her life is honorable.

When you quit spending any energy on how others live their lives it empowers you to further build your own. The only people you need to choose to cooperate with your vision are the ones who are directly in your life, i.e., a partner, children to an appropriate extent, etc. Other than that, no one needs to agree with you. So this whole need for other's approval is a wasted goose chase. Give it up.

You might be saying, "Wait a minute, aren't I going to end up a non-conformist if I dive in deep and accept this extraordinary way of life?" Yes, you are. That's an amazing thing. With the vast majority of people overweight, in debt, not in a healthy relationship, unhappy, and not fulfilled with their lives, don't you want to be a non-conformist? With only approximately 3% of people achieving their goals and just a shade more than that being independently wealthy, happy, and passionate, don't you want to be a non-conformist?

There is not a way to evaluate who is evolved past the minutiae phase in life i.e., routine daily necessities, you took my parking spot, blah, blah. People who have evolved understand what a profound experience life is that has nothing to do with daily minutiae. We are here to learn and to help each other. End of story.

You may think it matters tremendously who put the wet towel on the floor, or why your partner isn't pulling his weight. Honestly, those things are just noisy distractions to keep you from a meaningful life. An aimless life cares about all the distractions and low-level human activity to the point that their days run out before they have done anything of substance. With frustrated exhaustion, they vow tomorrow they will get around to what matters most.

I can't accept living like that anymore. People who are Living a Passionate Life! have gotten rid of the hectic craziness in their lives in favor of La Vida Loca (profound life experience). For some people that was a relatively quick and easy transition. For others it took a few years to get their lives to a more simplistic, responsible place which reflected what they love and allowed them to live passionately. People who have done this are in every part of the country. They are also in every socio-economic class and they are both genders. Hence, it is possible for every person to get the drama out of their lives.

Rather than waiting until all the drama is out of your life you can begin to simply focus on a more meaningful life first. Choose to avoid drama when it presents itself. Rather than get all enthralled in it, use a simple technique of "listen and leave." Listen for a brief amount of time, and then leave the situation for a positive choice. You don't have to get yourself involved just because your ego or other people want you to. None of us is responsible for solving everyone's problems. Resigning from that job can be very liberating and free up a ton of time for your passions.

If you have drama in your life, one of the best favors you can do for yourself is systematically eliminate it. Depending on what the drama is, it may take some time or even years to completely delete it. A decision to eliminate drama is powerful. Drama is the opposite of authentic passion, so the more drama you have in your life, the less authentic passion you will have. Hopefully that understanding will motivate you to create a focused action plan to eradicate it. Once the plan is in place, work the plan, but purposely focus as much energy as you can towards what you want in your life.

Remember people are drawn to drama because they desire dynamic connections in their lives. You don't have to meet that need with negative, false connections like gossiping or chaos, etc. especially when you have so many authentic ways to feel real passion in your life. Living with or entertaining drama is living by default rather than living on purpose.

The goal instead of drama is serenity. It is possible to allow other people to be in drama and choose to stay calm yourself. When you are serene, you don't react impulsively and over react. A state of Zen is a better place to make decisions and reflect on life.

The other category in Western culture that needs to be eliminated in order to live on purpose is chaos. We have created a culture that is overloaded from sun up to sun down, and start our children on that lifestyle as early as we can. Going from school to soccer to basketball to a theatre group three nights a week and filling the remaining four days with just as much activity with dinner in 12 minutes in the car while they change clothes and tell you about their day is not living for a child. That is a treadmill, going at such a fast pace that the children can't even take it all in let alone enjoy it. While they are growing they need down time. We have taught our children to not expect to be entertained every minute, as if boredom is the ultra enemy. Too many adults try to entertain themselves to death rather than learn to simply be.

In Western culture we push bigger, better, faster no matter who you are as if that is the best life for all people – one speed fits all. If you don't have a life of ambition where you are driving, living in, and vacationing past the visibly materialistic, you are perceived to be a slacker, leaving people to wonder what's wrong with you. If those things don't give you fulfillment, you have to be a confident non-conformist to go at your own pace on your own path.

There is a famous story that illustrates this so beautifully.

An American businessman was standing at the pier of a small coastal Mexican village when a small boat with just one fisherman docked. Inside the small boat were several large yellowfin tuna. The American complimented the Mexican on the quality of his fish.

"How long it took you to catch them?" The American asked.

"Only a little while." The Mexican replied.

"Why don't you stay out longer and catch more fish?"

Living a Passionate Life!

The American then asked.

"I have enough to support my family's immediate needs." The Mexican said.

"But," The American then asked, "What do you do with the rest of your time?"

The Mexican fisherman said, "I sleep late, fish a little, play with my children, take a siesta with my wife, Maria, stroll into the village each evening where I sip wine and play guitar with my amigos, I have a full and busy life, señor."

The American scoffed, "I am a Harvard MBA and could help you. You should spend more time fishing and with the proceeds you buy a bigger boat, and with the proceeds from the bigger boat you could buy several boats, eventually you would have a fleet of fishing boats."

"Instead of selling your catch to a middleman you would sell directly to the consumers, eventually opening your own can factory. You would control the product, processing and distribution. You would need to leave this small coastal fishing village and move to Mexico City, then LA and eventually NYC where you will run your expanding enterprise."

The Mexican fisherman asked, "But señor, how long will this all take?"

To which the American replied, "15-20 years."

"But what then, señor?"

The American laughed and said, "That's the best part. When the time is right you would announce an IPO (Initial Public Offering) and sell your company stock to the public and become very rich, you would make millions."

"Millions, señor? Then what?"

The American said slowly, "Then you would retire.

Lesson 4 – Living La Vida Loca!

Move to a small coastal fishing village where you would sleep late, fish a little, play with your kids, take a siesta with your wife, stroll to the village in the evenings where you could sip wine and play your guitar with your amigos..."

– Author unknown

It's easy to fall into that "bigger is better" mentality without thinking. Most people are not self-disciplined enough to step back and look at the meaning and purpose in their lives before they buy into what the mainstream is selling as the way to greatness. It takes a "pattern interrupt" to not jump on the bandwagon.

And it takes confidence to say "I'm living my life on my own terms and that is incredibly fulfilling."

For me that means I happily juggle two different types of businesses because it meets my need for variety. I keep them at a level that is best for my family first. A big paycheck less often is more exciting to me than a small steady paycheck. A flexible schedule is worth so much more to me than a steady paycheck with shiny awards. Working out of our house rather than an office in town allows me maximum time with my children and their needs. I would choose my self-directing over a micromanaging boss any day.

When you are willing to take the stance "I'm living my life on my own terms, and that is incredibly fulfilling" it doesn't matter if others understand.

I listened to that businessman's advice to the Mexican fisherman for three years. Everyone was telling me I had to sell online and get my writing and speaking to a multi-million dollar level before I could say I actually had a business. So that my family could have the life I wanted. I had the fortune to work closely with a multi-million dollar online businessman, multiple masterminds, attend conferences and worked with countless technical people. I believed them when they said "this is the only way to do this." Everything was about building the list of prospects in order to have a viable business.

When I came to the realization that this business is not me (I already knew I didn't have the technical brain) and stopped all of it, several people thought I was nuts. Some were harsh, threatening me with "You have no idea what you are giving up (close and personal access to the online multi-millionaire.) Anyone would give their right arm for that opportunity and you are just walking away." It didn't matter to me once I was clear that this was all crazy, like building for 15-20 years to get to an Initial Public Offering so I could have a life I already enjoy. Yes, I walked away.

I knew something many multi-millionaires don't, and that's the concept of "priceless." To spend the last years with my children at home trying to build a business, to maybe someday have millions of dollars that I never would have traded for what I already have right now, is crazy.

What you'll find is people who think that takes a lot of balls to say no to it all and they will respect you for getting out of the rat race, if it's not for you. Some may not be able to verbalize it. They'll make fun of some aspect of your life. But privately they'll respect you for doing your own thing. It doesn't matter if they agree or like your choices. It's your life.

Freedom is what allows us to not necessarily live a certain way the majority do. It takes someone self aware to step back and analyze their life periodically to make sure they are not just going with the flow, but rather doing what matters most each day. We can all find ourselves slipping back in the rat race now and then, and have to pull ourselves back so we can adjust.

For some reason, people think freedom means easy. Sometimes freedom can be really tough. If living your life on your own terms were easy, everyone would be doing it. You may decide one day that you are going to choose life on your own terms. It could take you a couple years to a decade to get it that way. An exceptional life is not for quitters.

Chaos is all the multi-tasking, scheduling to insanity, 100 priorities at once, letting everyone but you dictate your direction, more square footage and weeds than you can handle, and falling asleep on the couch because it's the first time that day you sat still for a few minutes. That doesn't even look like a life. It's a never-ending to-do list.

We move away from chaos by putting a laser focus on the things that really matter to us. The mission is to live your highest values on your own terms. Simplicity seems to be a core component for people who have been able to do that. Not the simplicity of living in a hut, but the simplicity of being who you want to be, doing what you want to do, and having the things you love in your life. Everything else can be let go.

Instead of an aimless life, you can ask, "How would I be living if I was living my best life?"

As you can tell from the four questions at the beginning of this lesson and the Mexican fishing village story, this is also a spiritual journey you are on. To be passionate just for the sake of being passionate is certainly a pleasurable personal experience, and yet it can be so much more if you look at it from a spiritual perspective.

God, The Divine, the Universe or whoever you believe is in charge didn't put us on this earth alone. That tells us something. We need each other and we are here to teach each other whether you realize that or not. For most of my adult life I have been very aware of the fact that we are here to teach each other. Perhaps until now you think of mentors, experts, and certified teachers as real teachers for you. Yet, I know others of you realize that everyone in your life is a teacher for you. That means your partners, children, boss, in-laws, neighbors, authors, brief encounters with strangers, the person who crashed into your car, the person who drives you nuts, the mother who is unconditionally loving, the person you can't get off your mind, elderly, and animals.

When you are open to people, experiences and opportunity like we talked about in chapter three and the things they can teach you, life becomes a much deeper and richer experience. All of a sudden, when someone or thing ticks you off you know to pay attention. There is a lesson for you. You may realize right away that an event in your life is a lesson and you can understand what it means for you. Other times the lesson might not be revealed for years. Lessons for your greater good are being sent to you. How effective you are at deciphering the lesson will determine your personal growth.

For myself, I have gotten to a place where I can reap the deeper, richer, better experience by looking back, present and forward as to what it all means in my life right now. I could take a day and map a timeline of the people, events and situations in my life with the decisions I made along with the consequences and understand what they all mean for me.

This ability didn't happen overnight. It came as I read different authors, listened to various teachers, watched my behavior and reactions as well as others, paid attention to what was working and what wasn't, and became more aware of the profound opportunity life is. Yes, one of my passions is personal development and this ability is the result of that passion. Just like most humans, my hindsight is often more clear.

Right now I can tell I am changing to a more spiritual awareness of the profound experience life is. Not the "I am a Christian, judge me against formal religion," but rather the "I realize I am a spirit having a human experience" type of changing. This reminds me when Mia, Dante and Lexi were little and were having a hard time understanding what it meant when we would say when you die the body stays here on earth and your spirit goes to heaven. I explained to them it was like a peanut. Your shell stays here and the good part of you, the peanut inside, is like your spirit and goes up to heaven. The shell is important while you're growing and protects you until you're ready, and then you don't need the shell anymore.

Part of my evolution and awareness about my life is that I have been a warrior most of my life. Born in a challenging situation on the wrong side of the tracks, I have spent my first 45 years fighting to get to the life I always wanted. And also the later part defending and protecting what I have created. None of this means I didn't live a passionate life until now. It is actually a strong indication of how passionate I was the whole time. It means there were times and situation in my life when I have had such fierce laser focus that no one could distract me. I did what I had to do to win the war no matter how hard it was or how long it took. That's

Living a Passionate Life!

why some closest to me say I have bigger balls than anyone they know.

I realize that warrior spirit has been very valuable to me and served me well. It will always be a part of me, as I am Native American. But I can step back and take a lesser expression of a warrior right now. Any time I need my warrior spirit I can call her forward and use it. So I honor my warrior, thank her for her service and need to let her go now.

When I first realized this I thought it was an age thing. For some reason I kept thinking women need to soften with age. A strong-willed, focused woman just didn't seem that attractive to me at later ages. Then I started questioning where was I getting this idea from? Well, there certainly is the harsh grandmother nobody thinks is "grandma" like. Then there is the "old battle axe" comment. I was feeling old and focusing on old, and didn't know why. Perhaps it was my 45th birthday. I maybe thought I had to quit acting so young. For the couple of months I was having these feelings I knew they weren't right, but I couldn't figure it out.

Then one morning while I was writing, it came to me. This feeling I was having was not about being old, but rather about the stage I was at in my life. It was time to let the strong, battling, defending and protecting warrior evolve into what I am feeling right now, which is compassion. Compassion is much softer than a warrior. I'll never forget the first time this was brought to my attention as a mother. It was 1999 and I was at a professional coaching conference where we each received coaching by another coach regarding a place we were stuck.

I was telling my coach about how excited I was to be married and a mother to Mia, who was 2 ½, and Dante who was 1. The joke with Andre was every time he went to videotape something we were doing I would cry because I was so happy. I thought I'd never get to experience that. So we would set our children on Santa's lap and Andre would give me a minute to choke back my tears. He'd ask if I was okay. I'd whimper out, "I'm just so happy" and he'd say "I know," as he gave me a big hug. I'm sure the hormones of having three babies in four years and lack of sleep didn't help either. I was emotionally charged and stuck in constant worry I would lose it all.

Of course I was blessed with a talented coach who said, "I want you to visualize that you are five years old and a little baby bird surprised you by landing in your hand while you are at the park. You are so thrilled that you start running as fast as you can to get home and show your mom. Your heart is racing and you are running so fast that you don't even realize, until you get home and open your hand, to show your mom the bird, that you have killed it from squeezing it too tight." That shocked me. I started sobbing and understood the lesson he wanted me to get.

He finished with "You have to be able to relax and enjoy the beautiful baby bird, choosing to sit on your open hand, without being afraid it will fly away."

I was a helicopter parent, intensely protecting and teaching, when my children were little. If anyone tried to harm my children, a mama bear came out that you don't want to meet.

Today my children don't need that warrior anymore, and I know it. I surprised myself when Mia first got her driver's license and I didn't have stress or worry about her taking off on her own. Andre couldn't believe it when just over a week after she got her license I said she could go to a basketball game at La Follette on a Friday night. The truth is, I hadn't thought about the fact that it was Friday night and the "beltline" is a traffic jam most adults like to avoid.

What I made my decision on was that Mia wanted to go and felt like she could do it. She had a good friend going with her who could help her navigate traffic and directions. When Andre questioned my judgment, I just said "I know she'll figure it out. She's a good driver and she's smart." She did end up getting lost but she ended up getting to the game. Both were valuable lessons for a 16-year-old driver.

So, on many levels I am aware I don't need the warrior spirit every day. What is coming up instead is a compassionate spirit which is actually funny. Honestly, I've known I am really compassionate my whole life. But for years I ignored and pushed down the compassionate part of me because I saw it as weak and was concerned people would take advantage of me. I have always been compassionate and unconditionally loving to my children. Yet at work and out in the world, I covered that up to protect myself. So when this feeling that compassion was now my main spirit came up, I knew it was time to look at compassion differently.

I misunderstood compassion. In reality, it takes a very strong person to be compassionate. Compassion means when you have abused me I cannot tolerate that, but I can also step back and understand why you do that. Compassion means I can't just care about my children, but rather I am concerned for all children. When I see someone homeless I don't yell at them "Get a job!" Instead I wonder how they become homeless – was it addiction, mental illness or job loss? And I also understand it could happen to me one day.

Lesson 4 – Living La Vida Loca!

I knew this feeling of moving towards compassion was right, it just felt vulnerable. I didn't really know how to be compassionate as my main way of being. What was I afraid of if I'm soft? Soft felt vulnerable to me. You can hurt me when I'm soft. If I fight, protect, and defend you can't get to my soft.

It made me remember when my mom, Pillar, and I had gone to a conference called Celebration in Chicago with all kinds of great authors presenting like Cheryl Richardson and Debbie Ford. Between sessions we visited the exhibit area where all the books and related items were being sold. What caught our eyes right away were two tables full of gorgeous crystal bracelets of all colors called Intentions Jewelry.

The point of the Intentions Jewelry was to choose one that "called" to you or felt right for you. At that time in my life the "Sekhmet" crystal bracelet seemed right for me. I wanted what the name described "She brings abundance of opportunities and limitless possibilities. As the goddess of the lions, she personifies inner and outer strength." My mom and I have very small wrists, so we both choose an extra small. At first I didn't notice anything.

Yet later that night my right wrist, the one wearing the bracelet, was incredibly painful on the back side of my wrist and traveling up the inside of my arm. My mom said "Maybe the bracelet is too tight and you should take it off." "No" I insisted. I wanted its magical powers. In the morning my arm had not gotten better, and my mom talked me into asking the jewelry maker about it. Right away Shareane Baff said, "Maybe it's too powerful for you. It is the goddess of the lions." She could see it was not too tight. Once again I insisted it was not too strong for me and I wanted to keep it. I conceded to exchange it for a size small and was determined "Shekmet" was the right one for me.

Fast forward to recently, and several people have told me the goddess of compassion is right for me. It made me realize the goddess of compassion was probably the right bracelet for me, but I wasn't ready to embrace it back then.

The popular way to transition from a warrior into a more compassionate spirit would be to just relax into it, but of course I didn't do that. I had just finished some big projects at work, our family had just transitioned to our first independent stage with Mia, and while this was great, it was still stressful. All of this was on my mind. One morning I was sitting in my favorite chair in the kitchen by the fireplace drinking coffee while Andre, Mia, Dante and Lexi were getting ready to leave for the day. Jose, our ten pound Yorkie, was perched on my chair right behind my head on my right side.

All of a sudden, Jose started barking like a rabid dog and flew off the chair to defend us from some perceived threat. Instantaneously, I shot up screaming my head off and spilled my hot coffee all over myself and the wood floor. I looked up to see my whole family looking at me with total confusion, right when tears started streaming down my face. I knew I had to get out of there. As soon as I got to my bedroom and closed the door I knew what was happening. My heart was racing, I couldn't stop crying and was sweating and shaking all over my body. It was post traumatic stress. It surprised me because for years that had not happened and I thought it was all done. Twice I have been physically and violently attacked, once from behind on my right side. To this day I can't stand it when anyone comes up behind me.

Lesson 4 – Living La Vida Loca!

It took me ten minutes to stop the physical reaction, even though I knew I was safe in my own home. My body had taken off without my mind and it took me a couple hours to shake off the surprise that came out of nowhere. By the afternoon I felt this massive stress relief and could laugh at my little dog being used to scare the crap out of me so I would chill out. That experience was a message that I was right about letting the warrior go and easing into compassion. If you don't get the subtle messages, a bigger message will come and get your attention until you get the lesson. That's how the life school works.

Do you pay attention to your life? I don't mean the watching your weight or bank account kind of attention. I mean the kind of attention where you actually listen to your life. Listening takes extra effort and attention. It is noticing anything you can about your life. When you listen you get feedback and awareness as to how your life is going and how you feel about it.

In 2010, I wanted to do something different for Lent and instinctually this idea of 40 Days of Listening came to me. I decided I was going to focus on listening more than talking as I am naturally a charismatic extrovert. Focusing on listening for 40 days would take me out of my usual mode. It would make me notice things that typically I might not notice when I am busy driving the conversation. A piece of leather tied around my right wrist, which looked like a bracelet, was my visual reminder to keep my commitment. With that type of a visual no one knew, whether I was at work or in my personal life. Only my family knew what I was doing.

This sacred time allowed me to pull back from my life and observe it for a little while. I paid attention to what I was hearing and also watched what was going on around me. It was easy to tell what I was happy with in my life and also where I was off track. At that point signs of grace really got my attention as well. You might be most familiar with the saying "I prayed to God to give me a sign so I would know what to do." Signs of grace can be a wide range of things from an idea that you get, to a connection you finally make, to $100 showing up when you really need it, the right person calling you out of the blues, etc.

My 40 Days of Listening also had an effect on my family because when I was quiet, the rest of the family had to step up and communicate more. It made me laugh that when I was quiet, my family finally wished I wasn't. Overall it was a very good and helpful experience.

Three years later, I decided to do 40 Days of Listening again for Lent. This time my primary purpose was to finish writing this book. I had gotten five chapters done earlier in the year and then just couldn't finish. Usually I can bang out a book in four months if I want to. This book was different. I was going to use intuition and my own thoughts to write it rather than doing any research to write a how-to type book. When I got to the point where I didn't know the answers, I had to wait until they came to me or I discovered them. So I figured 40 Days of Listening was just the focus and deadline I needed.

This 40 Days of Listening would be similar to the first time, except I used a sparkly crystal ring on the middle finger of my right hand to remind me of my commitment to listen. And I wanted to write at least 1,000 words a day. I would listen to my life primarily to hear what I should be writing.

I was pleasantly surprised at how much I had grown since the last time I did this practice. When I first began 40 Days of Listening, people's energy is what I noticed the most – particularly negative energy. It was overwhelming when it wasn't countered with my own positive energy. One area that felt overwhelming was the economy/political environment and the other was adults involved in youth athletics. I chose to not get emotionally involved in both of these during this time. It worked fine, since I didn't have to involve myself. I could tune out the media and quietly videotape the games while I reminded myself to stay detached.

Listening is not just with your ears, of course. So when I was at the bookstore looking for something to read and couldn't find anything in my usual sections, I kept looking in the back of the bookstore. There on an end display looking at me like, "Hello, I've been waiting for you" was a book I was excited to read. After I bought the book, I remembered I had heard about this book months ago and it wasn't published yet.

I would journal about something before bed and in the morning while I was sitting in my favorite chair by the fireplace, I would get an idea that was the answer I was looking. Something would come on the television or a song on the radio that would give me another clue. If I asked someone about the clue, they would add some insight that helped me think about it in a different way.

When I am deep into writing my children are used to me looking at their faces while I think. They don't even say "What?" anymore. They just know Mom's trying to figure something out. Their faces are a wonderful place to jog my thoughts. Just as new environments are a great place to "listen" because they awaken your senses. Running on the elliptical (because it was winter) helps release any stress or tension. After I'd showered, my energy was in a fresh new place to begin again. Even your mailbox, electronic or physical, can deliver "messages" you need to listen to.

One place people don't tend to "listen" closely to is our feelings. 40 Days of Listening is a perfect time when you pull back from the social pleasantries and can pay attention to how your feelings feel to you. What happens in your body when you encounter someone or a situation? Do you tense up? Are you excited? Where did that headache or stomachache come from? Why do you feel like eating and especially that food you are craving right now? When we don't address our feelings is usually when we have trouble in our lives. Everything happening in our bodies, which includes feelings, is trying to tell us something if we would listen.

At about day 16 of listening I started thinking about my silly fear of happiness. Sadly, I was getting snarky feedback that some women were mistaking my Living a Passionate Life! as I am a pampered wife. My first reaction was of defensiveness, feeling like I needed to let everyone know I had worked really hard to get to this stage of my life. Then I remembered it was a lesson I was getting. I changed my attitude to gratitude for the lesson because it's all part of me daring to let you see my happiness and not caring if you hate me for it.

When someone reacts to you, the vast majority of the time, it's not even about you. They are reacting to something going on with them; hence, it's not personal. What I learned from my 40 Days of Listening is to step back and take some space before I react. When I do that I can have compassion for the person, even if I don't like what they're doing. I can also leave it and not get involved, even when socially that might seemed rude.

But I saw something when I was offended by anyone referring to me as a pampered wife. Remember I defensively tried to justify that I worked hard for everything I got. That's true. I did work really hard. Yet what I saw was a false belief. Why did I think happiness can't come easy? It hasn't been my experience, but that doesn't mean it's not true. And furthermore, how much of that was me preventing it anyway? What I have found along the way are plenty of people who control or prevent their happiness. That's the funny thing about isolation. When we keep things private we often think we are the only one dealing with it. Then when we open up, we find there are plenty of other people trying to learn that lesson too.

Since we are on the topic, learning that it isn't anyone's job to make you happy is also important. That means it's not my spouse's job to make me happy. Traditional marriage may make you think it is, but that is really unfair to the spouse. Yes, they should be a loving and considerate partner but, it is a selfish expectation to put the responsibility on him. *Sacrifice your life so that I can be happy, and any time that I am not happy I get to blame you* – does that seem right? It's an easy excuse but it puts the responsibility on the wrong person.

It certainly isn't my children's job to make me happy, although plenty of parents treat their children as if it is. It's not my friends' job. It's not our parents' job or your boss's. There is only one person who is responsible for your happiness, and that's you. Once you take responsibility for that, you can't help but look at your choices, decisions and consequences differently. The bottom line is that happiness is an internal choice. It is fleeting. It will come and go. You can experience it every day if you want to. If you lighten up it will come more often. Happiness will surprise and excite you. In the next chapter we will dive into happiness in more depth, and I promise you will enjoy it.

Life is continually teaching us. That is part of the profound experience. It can be an exhilarating experience if you allow it and participate. Learning to hear what your intuition is telling you can change your life. Every person has this intuition. The difference is not everyone pays attention or gives this feedback credibility. Intuition is instinctually knowing something, often without proof it is correct. First it takes a willingness to notice it, and second, it takes faith to trust or know your intuition is right. But you can see from the examples of me paying attention to my intuition, I have changed my life numerous times as well as written this whole book using it.

In our hectic digital world we are rarely taking time for our mind to be quiet and listen anymore. It can be difficult to disconnect, and yet there are opportunities numerous times a day to quiet the mind and listen. So much of finding quiet time comes in instilling new habits. We will talk about this more in the next chapter, but some easy ways are getting up ten minutes early to quietly set your intention for the day. Leave the television off in the morning. Twice during the day, leave the radio off in the car. Spend ten minutes after a meeting to ask yourself how you felt about the meeting.

These changes may feel good to you right away as a pleasant reprieve from your racing mind, or they may seem difficult and not effective. Stay committed. It will work as intuition always does when we allow it. I am not saying you will like everything your intuition will point out to you. Part of intuition's job is to warn you before it's too late. Intuition wants to help guide you throughout your life. Intuition is like a muscle that will get stronger as you use it. As you gain confidence in being able to hear your intuition, it will become more valuable to you.

Isn't our experience of living amazing? When you really think about what it means to have life and go through this experience, it is exciting. The sooner we realize how it all works, the quicker we can maximize this opportunity. All of the distractions just keep you out of the profound game that is going on around you.

Sadly, the vast majority of people never understand that life is a profound opportunity. They believe the ego's trap that life is hard, we are supposed to struggle, and then we die. It's easy to determine who is living this way – just listen to what they talk about. They will be pessimists who tell you how much life sucks and they will always blame others rather than taking accountability for their actions or mentality. They will also be the external people who are affected with the three accidental teachings of the ego you learned in lesson one. They hold grudges for years and don't understand the concept that forgiveness is for them, not the person they are forgiving. All of this will keep you from a profound experience.

Perhaps the most amazing thing is the fact that we can grow and change whenever we don't like the way our lives are going. We also don't have to believe that life has to be hard. When you clear away all of the minutiae, chaos and toxic energy we talked about, life actually becomes simple. Simple to the affect that your values and purpose can drive your life while you also enjoy each day – simple because it is easy to see what you say "yes" and "no" to. And mostly profound because of the once in a lifetime opportunity it is to be alive. You know you were allowed to come here at this exact time with a specific number of days, a unique purpose, and free will to decide what you would do with it. Isn't that *La Vida Loca*!?

Lesson 5
Experiencing Life!

Would you like to know what people regret on their deathbed? Why would you want to know about such anti-climatic things in a book about passion? What would the benefit of that be? The answer is so you can avoid them, of course. If you knew what the top five regrets were, would you do anything different to avoid them? Maybe you think it depends on what they are. Bronnie Ware, a nurse who worked for years with the dying, wrote a list of the top five regrets people say aloud on their deathbed. The list gained so much popularity that she wrote the book *The Top Five Regrets of The Dying*. Their answers could be clues as to how to do a better job at this profound game of life we are all playing.

The first regret was, "*I wish I'd had the courage to live a life true to myself, not the life others expected of me.*"

When they looked back over their lives, this is what they saw as the biggest regret. This meant they had dreams that they never fulfilled as much as it meant they lived their lives for others more than themselves. Most of these people admitted they hadn't fulfilled even half of their dreams. And worse yet, they had to die knowing it was because of choices they had made. A caution they gave was *don't wait*. If you wait until your health is compromised, it could be too late to try to live a life true to yourself.

What's so hard about living a life true to yourself? As you can tell from the regret, it probably means hurting people in the process. That might be telling your parents you aren't interested in the career they think is best for you. It might mean leaving a marriage that you have not been happy in for more than a decade. It might be saying no to your children because what they want doesn't go with your values. It could also be going after a career you have always wanted, traveling abroad for a year, or downsizing to get out of the rat race.

Why do we feel so pulled by what other people want from us to the point that they get more say in our lives then we do? We all do this at various times and in certain situations. Certainly we can't only care about what is true to our authentic selves or we would have to be completely alone. But knowing that not being true to yourself is the biggest regret might motivate your confidence to let people see who you really are.

It took me until my 40s before I became who I

wanted to be. It did frustrate and annoy me that it took that long, but then my coaching friends always remind me some people never get to that place. Yet I will also say it's a great feeling to be comfortable with who you are and run your life from an internal perspective instead of external. Too many people run their life by committee, meaning they have a need to please others before themselves.

A large part of the problem is difficulty with people-pleasing, especially for women who are taught to be selfless because everyone else needs them to be. While there are certainly overly self-indulged people, some people need to learn to choose themselves first more often. Being true to yourself as a person and going after at least some of your dreams is the only way to avoid regret number one.

The second regret was, "I wish I hadn't worked so hard."

That response came from every male respondent. Women regretted this too, but not every woman. Most of the respondents were old, and many of the women weren't breadwinners, which might have been why. When people who regretted it looked back, they saw they missed their children's growing up and companionship with their spouse.

Usually there are two reasons people become workaholics. The first is being driven by money, and the second is to avoid the rest of your life as you feel the best about yourself at work. Often, workaholics don't notice until it's too late, i.e. their spouse wants a divorce, the children are grown and leaving the house, or there is a major health issue threatening their life or they die of a heart attack at work.

Work, or having some way to support yourself, is

important in a capitalist country. There is no way to get around the financial factor. But workaholics usually have a compulsive need to avoid the rest of their life. Work is not often where any of us have our profound life experiences. Apple's Steve Jobs, for example, accomplished what he did at the expense of his personal life and that was very evident in his biography.

Have you ever heard anyone say they wish they had worked more when they were on their deathbed?

Knowing this regret, would you be willing to cut back on some of your expenses so you don't have to work so much? If not, are you willing to find more time to put towards your family? If you are working too much, what are you missing? When you tell yourself the truth, is it worth what you're missing? You're still breathing so it's not too late to change it.

The third regret was, "I wish I'd had the courage to express my feelings."

In order to keep the peace, many people suppressed their feelings. It's unhealthy to keep feelings bottled up in the body. Illnesses can actually be developed relating to bitterness and resentment. One way or another, feelings have to come out. Doesn't expressing your feelings seem like a simple change you can make so you don't have this regret? It might take some time to get comfortable or you may need to start privately, like working out your feelings in your journal first.

One easy way to diffuse emotions when you are sharing them with others is to use "I" instead of the accusatory "you." "I feel ____ when you _____." Instead of "You always ____." The problem with the second one is your real feelings are masked because you're attacking the thing that triggers you, not what's behind it. Another phrase some people are afraid to use is "I don't like it when ____." Chances are, the person you are speaking to might not have known. Don't forget to express the positive too. "I feel appreciated when ____."

Did you notice this regret ties into the first regret? I am afraid to be who I really am and express my feelings because others may not like it. And did you notice what probably feels bad about that is you may be manipulating others and yourself in order to not be true to yourself and express your feelings? You are dating the woman of your dreams who wants children, and you tell her "Sure, I want to be a dad," when the truth is years later, as a dad, you knew that lifestyle wasn't for you. The bad feeling is often feeling like an impostor in your own life. Perhaps some of the hardest feelings to express are when we have changed over time. "I don't love you anymore," "I resent you because you are so self-indulged," "I feel inspired to (major life change)," or "I have forgiven and feel love for the person/people who have hurt me the most."

Sometimes the discomfort in expressing our feelings involves people we want and don't want in our lives. Anger is another feeling people try to keep hidden. If they'd learn to properly express it, pain is the real feeling they are not seeing. When we don't identify and express our feelings it creates as many problems as we might think it solves. Human beings are the only species who hold on to years of torment over a feeling that occurred twenty years ago. Dogs don't relive what they did wrong day after day.

The fourth regret was, "I wish I had stayed in touch with my friends."

I believe this regret leans to the idea that no one

wants to die alone. Many on their deathbed want kinship and support going through the final process of life. Once those experiencing this regret realized the full benefits of old friends, it was often too late to track them down. Often they became busy with their own lives, and golden friendships disappear. The deepest regret came from not giving these friendships the time and effort they deserved.

This regret surprised me a bit. I would have thought family relationships would be a regret over friends, but given the results I can hope there weren't as many regrets about family. It seems easy to understand this regret if you have a family, as those demands are seen as necessities and friendship a luxury. I think the regret comes from thinking our family is everything when children eventually go on to their own lives. Too many marriages end in divorce – then what do you have? You even hear contemporary phrases like "Husbands may come and go but friends are forever," and "The best time to make friends is before you need them." So I can see the regret.

How do your friendships look today? Do you have as many or few as you like? Are you cherishing them? Do you need to improve any of them? Is there something you need to say or not say to deepen those friendships? How could you be a better friend? How would you like to have friends at your current stage of life? You can appreciate friends if this regret speaks to you.

This regret reminds us that all that is left in the final weeks is love and relationships. It is not the details that consume us on a daily basis as those will soon be a mute point.

The fifth regret was, "I wish that I had let myself be happier."

Lesson 5 – Experiencing Life!

What the regretters wished they knew sooner was that happiness is a choice. They had gotten too comfortable in their set routines and challenges of life – which affected them emotionally and physically. Pessimism can develop if you're focusing on the wrong things in life, and we all know pessimists are choosing to not be happy. Even if you're not a pessimist you might fear change. Bronnie found "Fear of change had them pretending to others, and to their selves, that they were content, when deep within, they longed to laugh properly and have silliness in their life again."

So it seems time to drink in the sunshine, laugh at your mistakes, go with your impulses, eat ice cream for dinner, kiss your man's neck like you mean it, let your dog on the furniture, relax and be silly with your children, smile to yourself when you find a sign of grace, enjoy your senses, be good to yourself like someone you love, and above all allow and choose happiness.

Again, this regret surprised me by how sadly common it was and hence, why this book is so important. I have known for years that happiness is a choice and ever since then I have been happier. My learning came from my thought "You can't trust happiness." What was wrong was my expectation that happiness should be trusted. "If I trust you, happiness, you can't go away." Well, I learned that was an unfair expectation and happiness doesn't work that way. External happiness does ebb and flow with life as you know. No one has mastered a happy-for-all-of-life existence yet. There are tears, anger and unpleasant emotions which have been said are needed to really appreciate the good times. I certainly think I do appreciate without needing the occasional disaster to remind me. But I'm also clearly aware I am not in charge of many things in life.

And most recently, I have learned the Eastern form of internal happiness that allows you to be in control any time you want to be. I'm not going to lie and tell you it's easy all the time. It is a choice even in the middle of the biggest drama of your life. What I have learned to do is appreciate the fact that this tough challenge is a lesson that will allow me to eventually be happier and also this day or hour is not completely bad as I can enjoy some of the small pleasures in life. Like fresh air or a good night's sleep. Looking at my children always helps me keep the bigger picture in mind and makes me smile.

So after all of that, theses five simple keys might be part of the answer to a good life.

1. Live an authentic life.
2. Keep work in balance.
3. Express feelings.
4. Cultivate friendships.
5. Choose to be happy.

What's beautiful about this life experience is each of us gets to craft the art of living the way we want to and just like art, an original is so much better than a mass replica. So this list might not be the exact blueprint that lends itself to your ideal expression. Mold it, delete it, add to it, and twist it until it looks beautiful to you. And when you get your art of living to the place that takes your breath away – embrace it fully!

We are an adrenaline junkie nation that often doesn't think it's fully alive unless fireworks are going off in our minds. And if the pleasure is of the milder variety, we barely notice or feel satisfied. When we talk

Lesson 5 – Experiencing Life!

about experiencing life, the bucket list idea comes to mind right away. A bucket list, as you know, is the almost impossible triumphs of a lifetime that only count if hardly anyone can do them kind of adventures. The bucket list actually ignites the fight-or-flight mechanism, which is a manic state. To be in a manic state a few times over a lifetime doesn't hurt anything. But expecting the bucket list mania to be what it feels like to truly experience life is short-sighted. One easy way to experience more in life is to quit thinking they have to be manic moments to count.

Always looking for the next quest sets you up for a roller coaster. The highs feel really high at the peak of the quest, and the lows feel really low like life is not worth living. Chasing life is different than experiencing life. Drug addicts know what it means to chase the next high, and it's incredibly difficult to give up chasing. Chasing your next romantic relationship, chasing skinny, chasing fame, chasing accolades, chasing, chasing, always chasing and never feeling satisfied. Chasing wears you out a whole lot faster, often feeling like a wild goose chase with no substance. Chasing it like the imagery of me squeezing that baby bird because I wanted happiness so badly rather than being able to let it gently sit on my hand if it chose to.

You might be asking the question, *how would I know if I'm chasing or experiencing life,* because I do attempt quests. Intent is the way you can tell. Are you so driven with your hair on fire that you don't enjoy the journey? Do you think it's a completely lost cause if you don't get to the summit, or do you know there are lessons and richness in every assignment we take on? Are you open to whatever happens along your quest, or will you only accept the exact outcome you find acceptable? Do you not feel alive unless you are chasing (the high is more important than anything else)?

On the other hand, experiencing life is enjoying the entire journey. Experiencing life is the whole smorgasbord of life. It's the little moments and big moments, but mostly the deep moments. What I'm talking about is the richer, deeper, better experiences that are possible for every one of us if we want them. Isn't that silly, really? We have lived this long and yet perhaps we have not learned how to get the most out of life.

Would you like to embrace life at a deeper, full sensory level? It wouldn't involve multi-tasking. It does involve being fully present and learning to use all of your senses to your advantage. While you are watching a movie, do you only use your eyes and ears or do you also feel the movie with your heart? After you have been at a party can you remember what people were wearing? What their face looked like? Why you might not have liked someone? Can you find your way around without street signs? What exact color blue was the sky tonight? Where is your favorite place to sit and relax? Do you like a lot of noise or mostly quiet environments?

What do you want more of in your life? Make a list. How can you make it happen? Make your list more interesting by separating it into as many categories as you can think of, like: What do you want more of in your life that is free? What do you want more of in your life that is from another culture? What do you want more of in your life that is fun? What do you want more of in your life that is usually overlooked? You can change this question to the opposite and also ask as many of these types of questions you can think of.

Experiencing life doesn't have to be all serious. I

have a list of things I feel my children need to know how to do or experience before they leave home. Two items on that list are run out of gas and use the laundromat. Yes, I really let our SUV run out of gas on Highway M to see what Mia, Dante and Lexi would do. I was right there, but only gave them feedback on their ideas. By the time we had returned the gas can and were back on the road, they knew what to do more vividly than me telling them and I'm certain they will remember it. It is not that we have to experience everything in order to have an understanding or learn the lesson, but the ones we experience have a more lasting effect on us.

Passionate people know themselves. What's important to know is where you've been, where you're going, what you like, what you don't like, your strengths and your weakness. Learning more about all of those helps you create the life you want. It is highly valuable information if you know how to use it to your advantage.

In 2006, writer and editor Larry Smith came up with an idea that really intrigued me. The challenge was to come up with a six-word memoir. In other words, use six words to describe your entire life. That is shocking! However long your life has been, can you imagine capturing it well in only six words? The concept of the six-word memoir was so interesting.

Here are some examples from O magazine: "Still fit into my high school earrings" – Kimberly Kilroy, 53. "Every 20 years, I reinvent myself" – Wahana Vellutini, 83. "Might as well eat that cookie" – Paula Deen, 65. "I dance daily, watched or not" – Olivia Whitman, 32. "Forever entertained by the universe's humor" – Val Morini, 27.

What would your six words be? That's a big assignment. What six words exactly depict what you are about? It would be easier if you come up with six words for each decade to reflect where you have been. I'm sure that would be an interesting assignment in itself. Perhaps it would be easier to do that first and then condense those down into your final six words. As a personal development junkie, it's refreshing when I come across a new idea.

I had to take the long approach to this assignment. I started with what are the main lessons I learned from 0-18 years of age and then did 19-present. A memoir is "a record of events written by a person having intimate knowledge of them and based on personal observation." My six-word memoir at this point of my life is, "Making art of what I've learned." Art is self expression. My art is specifically my Sofia Michaels books that capture what I have learned from life and it is also my children, our custom-built home, my public speaking presentations, my creative ideas I put into motion, the way I dress, etc.

What's your personal observation of your life so far? Give the six-word memoir a try and see what ideas it brings up for experiencing life. You might also like to create one for today going forward. What six words would you like to describe your life? How would you go about implementing those six words? It's important that the words inspire you. The words are not a mission, but rather a way of being in the world. This is more personal and lets everyone know what you are all about.

Beginning with the idea for the first Sofia Michaels book, I made a commitment that they would be a cathartic journey of my life and in doing that they would be helpful to me and hopefully inspiring to others. The writing of each one would have a very specific purpose that was tremendously challenging to me. The first one had a purpose of overcoming my past and was written in an intimate journal style. The second book was a "how-to" feel strong capable, and make your own dreams come true.

The writing of this third book in this series is not about getting it done or rushing through it. It's about enjoying every piece of time and letting the writing take its own pace and introduce me to where I need to be going. By this book, my writing has become much more of an intuitive creative process rather than a how-to. When I committed to make this book even more intimate than the last two, friends couldn't imagine how I could do that. What I meant was I am going to let readers into my mind and see how it works without worrying about their reactions. Pretty intimidating, right?

I'm freely leaning forward on the edge of a cliff or surfboard with my arms wide open, letting the writing take me where it wants. My two previous Sofia Michaels books have been written in a different voice than this one, as I let the subject choose the words, tone and intensity. My writing is playing with me much like I'm sure paints play with my mom or the piano plays with my mother-in-law. So, in true commitment, this book has completely switched direction on me more than once. My job as the author was to just go with it and accept that where it takes me is exactly where the book needed to be. That even meant pulling me to Mexico in the final week of writing. You'll hear more about that in the final lesson, Almost Heaven.

As an author, you have to experience life if you're

going to write about it. If I just sat home on the couch, how would I be able to evolve as an author in order to help you grow too? Andre and I had been on a trip to Florida when I got an offer to attend an on-line marketing conference in California two weeks from then. The offer came from Rich Greene, one of my mastermind group members, and whenever I am starting to feel old or comfortable I know I have to take a risk. The conference wasn't in my comfort zone as it was for online marketing. I had never met Rich in person before, as our group meetings were all via conference calls. That could have been a little dicey. Rich was professional, a gentlemen and has become a good friend. However, professionally, at the time it was all a leap of faith for me. You can either live scared or do business. As is my style, I set up a treat at the end of the conference to motivate me through it.

Bryan Weber, one of my former marketing students, was working for Disney in California. Bryan was one of my favorite students and such a neat person. I actually told him at 17, "If I ever have a son, I want him to be just like you." Bryan was so polite, had a good relationship with his parents, was well-liked, funny, thoughtful and all the girls thought he was adorable (although I wasn't looking for that one.) To be able to say that about a teenage boy is a wonderful thing. So you can tell Bryan was someone special.

I hadn't seen Bryan in more than ten years, although I often wondered how he was doing. What was so important about this incredible story was our adventure started at Disney in Florida. As you have heard about in *Pretendia,* I took Bryan and seventeen other high school marketing students to Disney University during spring break. After college Bryan

Lesson 5 – Experiencing Life!

went to work for Disney in Florida so that was neat, but the story doesn't end there. Bryan has always been committed to experiencing life. Eventually he left everything but his romantic partner to drive to California and live out of his car until he landed a job at Disney.

I had shown Bryan Disney, and now more than a decade later he would show me his Disney. So you see, come hell or high water, I had to make it to Bryan. And high water came, a couple times. I hadn't ridden a train since I was three years old, so I listened to the travel agent when she told me what train to take and bought my ticket before I left Wisconsin. At 10:35 p.m. when I hailed a cab after getting off the train I was told I was an hour away from my hotel. The driver said I should go back to the ticket office and get on a train before the station closed at 11:00 p.m. My cell phone was dying and I needed to call the hotel to let them know I was still coming, which I was stressed about. At the ticket office, surprise, they hadn't punched my ticket so I was told to just get back on the train. With 15 minutes to spare, I ran into the bathroom looking for an outlet to charge my phone. There were no electric outlets out in the train station. The only one I could find was directly under the water pipe on the sink. In Wisconsin that would be a major code violation, but I was desperate and a little panicked about running out of battery traveling alone.

I plugged in and planted my feet a shoulder width apart like I knew what I was doing. I proceeded to eat my Subway sandwich over the sink like that was normal with my eyes constantly scanning my right and left side like I was on defense for basketball. There were two ladies pacing around and one in the stall who were all talking to themselves like they were crazy. The ones I could see appeared to be homeless and next to me was a lady of the evening getting ready for work. She had a chunky gold dollar sign with rhinestones around her neck, a micro-mini skirt, tight shirt, and fishnet stockings and was spraying perfume between her legs. I felt like I was going to lose it when she leaned over and asked "Are you looking for love tonight?" My knees, thighs, calves and butt clenched to try and hold my ground and I tossed my head in her direction as nonchalant as I could manage and calmly said "Nah, I'm good."

I made it another 30 seconds, unplugged my phone, grabbed my luggage and hightailed it out of there as fast as I could. I saw a service counter and rushed to it. At the service counter, they said I looked clean enough to go in Starbucks and ask them if I could use an outlet for the remaining five minutes I had before the last train. I realize that's not fair discrimination, but I was desperate.

Just after midnight I arrived at my Disney hotel that all felt very familiar. Safe, clean and fun, yet I still couldn't sleep. I had slept about two hours a night throughout the conference and this night was no different. At 10:30 a.m. I decide I better see which streets I should take to walk to Disney Studios for my interview with Bryan. What?! I am within walking distance of Disneyland, not Disney Studios! I quickly call the front desk and they say, "Oh, yeah. Disney Studios are in Burbank, about an hour's drive." It felt like the top of my head blew off in shock as I panicked about how I was going to get there in time, and I swore I would not drive in California. But there was no way I was going to be this close to seeing Bryan and have to cancel.

Lesson 5 – *Experiencing Life!*

The front desk was very accommodating as they tried to call around to find me a shuttle service that was not too late or a million dollars. Dominick called me back and gently told me there was no way to get there but driving. He had arranged a car service and promised me Fernando would take good care of me at the car rental place. During the five minute ride over there, my mind kept running with "How am I going to do this?" The minute I stepped on the parking lot I spotted a royal blue Mustang convertible.

As I spoke with Fernando, I felt like a teenager begging to borrow the car as I knew he had to trust me. When he asked me what kind of a car I was thinking of I remember my Women 101 training, *ask for what you want,* and said "I'll take the blue Mustang convertible at the budget daily rate and I want to drop it off at the LA airport without charge tonight." Fernando hooked me up with all the extras and programmed a GPS for the price I wanted. We took a quick picture as I post my adventures on Facebook, and even though it was cold, the top had to go down.

To tell the truth, I was scared crapless to pull out on the California highway and drive in an expensive car that wasn't mine. The highway was massively busier and tremendously faster paced that what I was used to. Cars didn't seem to care who you were or where you thought you were going – they were going where they wanted – period. Move it or lose it was the energy, and I quickly had to get in the game. Fernando had given me one piece of advice about the GPS, as I don't use one of those either – "Follow the purple line." I had no clue where I was or where I was going. All I could do was follow the purple line and thankfully I'm visual.

I was going for it because I had to make it to Bryan.

Living a Passionate Life!

Within a couple minutes I felt like I was playing a video game switching gears and weaving in and out of traffic like I belonged there, as my long hair was whipping around in my face. Soon after I had the music cranking and was absolutely enjoying the adrenaline, fresh air and sunshine. To my thrill there were no accidents, and I made it in enough time to park at Starbucks with time to spare.

I could have gone inside Starbucks, but why would I? I can do that at home. So for a half hour I sat in the car, let the music play loud, wrote a blog and when anyone walked by looking at me weird I shouted "I'm from Wisconsin!" with a big smile on my face.

When Bryan came walking up to meet me at the security gate he looked gorgeous. Gorgeous became I hadn't laid eyes on him in so many years and he looked confident, sharp and totally in love with his vibe in life. It is so wonderful as an educator to see your students grow into themselves in such an amazing way. It just made me happy to see him here in this setting as Manager, Signature Programs for Corporate Citizenship for Disney. That young man from Waunakee, Wisconsin had certainly made something of himself.

As we sat down for lunch I felt a little awkward at first as we began to catch up and I had to stop for a moment to ask, "You're at least 28, aren't you?" I laughed when he told me he's in his early thirties so I could relax. You'd never find me pulling a Mary Kay Letourneau. This is a little weird with all my adult students turned friends at first. But I was so intrigued by the conversation we were having that I soon let my teacher guard down and drank up everything he was saying.

As Bryan walked me to the car, he was very much a

Lesson 5 – Experiencing Life!

gentlemen and that warmed my heart. He said, "Isn't it amazing that this is the same place Walt Disney himself used to work?" and I froze in place as I immediately looked at my former student, and now good friend, in that awe for a moment. To be where some of the most creatively passionate people work blows my mind. I quickly take it all in like it was going to go away in an instant. The fact that I am here experiencing all of this by the pure blessing that Bryan chose my marketing class as a 17-year-old young man brings me pure gratitude and excitement. I'm so happy for him and all he is being in the world and doing. He had a dream and stuck with it which so many people don't do.

This trip was really experiencing life and I'm glad I could bring you along to show you what that feels like. Remember, I told you to be open to people, experiences and opportunities in lesson three. This trip is an example of how you do that. Meeting new people, trying new skills, getting out of your comfort zone, enjoying friends, reminded me of one more experience that happened on this trip.

At the conference, Rich had executive tickets, which meant he was tied up with extra meetings and working meals. That meant I was on my own to meet new people and find lunch dates. This kind man introduced himself to me the first day and asked if I wanted to go to a Thai restaurant with Susan Hyatt, an author/expert on corporate philanthropy, and I happily accepted. We had the most enjoyable conversations about what we were writing and how we got onto that path in the first place. The guy had this totally funny title for a book called *Spankings from the Universe.* It was funny because we can all relate to lessons we've learned along the way. But as we talked, I was shocked as to what the journey of his book was really all about.

He was Middle Eastern and believed religiously in karma. He had been warned repeatedly by spiritual leaders to give all of his money away to escape the karmic debt placed on his money seven generations back. At first he didn't listen, and his wife had a near-death car accident. Then his house was damaged and after four months of seeking spiritual guidance he decided to listen. He transferred the title of their home to his wife and gave every bit of his money away. What a story! I couldn't help but say, "I don't mean to be disrespectful, as I realize these are your religious beliefs, but what if they were wrong?"

He lethargically responded, "I couldn't risk it." Talk about a story that should be written. I couldn't wait to read it in two months when he was supposed to be done. He was having some trepidation, as his father would never forgive him for putting his sinful ways in print. (Almost a year later, I haven't seen the book.)

The next day he invited two more fascinating people to join our little group. One was Len Branson, who shockingly resembles Sir Richard, but I decided I wasn't going to be tied to titles as we were connecting so strongly as human beings. I'm sure he gets asked that all the time. He was a documentary film maker of Superwise Me *The Experiment: What Happens When You Listen To Your Heart* and founder of Superwise Love Foundation. The other person was who Len calls his beloved, Akua Auset. She was an artist and holistic beauty advisor whose essence radiated beauty. Years ago she had a naming ceremony and Akua Auset was chosen for herself which means sweet messenger. For an author the food was wonderful, and the company was even more delicious. We sat and traded stories, thought-provoking ideas and a blissful energy until the restaurant closed.

I am not able to have adventures like that every day, but they really remind me how even in our daily lives we can be more present and engaged in each interaction and person we get to have time with. Maybe that's not even true. I try to approach each day like it's a new adventure and perhaps this reminds me to surrender to it rather than try harder because these were all easy interactions when I allowed them.

The other thing I always notice when I take some time to reflect is how fear controls so much of our decisions and life experiences. *I can't travel alone, I have to wait until my children don't need me, if I spend the money we'll have an emergency and I'll end up in the poorhouse, my boss would never let me, she can do that, but not me...*

Fear comes from your ego, and it's trying to scare you in place. If the ego can keep you fearing things it can control you. The only way to deal with fear is to let fear pass through you. For a few brief moments, it will feel like the fear is going to kill you, like walking through the fire of life. But if you can breathe through it and keep telling yourself "I can handle this" *or* "This too shall pass", it will go away much faster than anything else you could do. When fear shows up in your life, you can decide if you want to lean in when you want to get involved and lean back when you don't. "Let it be" is an Eastern practice where you can notice something you don't like and just let it be there. We don't have to react and get emotionally involved all the time.

If you want to make art of what you live, you have to surrender from fear and surrender to being spiritually and intuitively guided in your life. Trusting that the universe is taking care of you. That means you can't have your feet on the gas and the brake at the same time. You will have to get your foot off the brake and believe you won't crash. Trusting that the universe is taking care of you doesn't mean nothing bad will happen to you again. It means that what does happen will be for your greater good, even if you don't understand it at the time.

In recent years, I have become a big believer in that concept. I know everything I have ever gone through was to help me grow into the person I am today. Today is preparing me for the future. I really don't have regrets, because a regret means you wished it never happened. I've made plenty of bad decisions and unfortunate things have happened, just like everyone else. Yet to remove an element or two would change what I enjoy today, so I wouldn't do it. People are often surprised when they hear me say that given what some of the circumstances were.

Today I look at everything as an assignment I signed up for. Some of them kick my behind badly. Others are so tremendously blissful I can't believe I am fortunate enough to have them in my life. It's all important in the grand scheme of things, and I can't see the grand map. I have to have faith and trust.

My job in surrendering and allowing my life to be guided is to listen and take action, like I told you about in my 40 Days of Listening practice. One of the hardest for me to surrender, in order to be led, was my attachments. I think everyone has things they are overly attached to. Attachments can be actual things, people, or even ideas. My attachments that were hardest to surrender were our home, as I was committed to stay at least until Lexi graduated, my wedding ring, my marriage, and our children. I'm sure the first thing you are wondering is did I get rid of any of those things. I didn't, so let me explain surrendering.

As you know, I moved a lot when I was growing up and even wrote about this fierce commitment to stay in this home until all three of our children graduate. Along the way Andre wasn't as emotional about our home as I was, although he really likes it. He's asked a few times if I was ready to downsize. My answer was always no. Our home was my Achilles heel, and I had kept this dream of security alive for more than ten years. Meaning I thought I would literally die if we lost our home for any reason. It was 100% emotional for me. I didn't feel that way about our two previous homes, so clearly you can see this attachment was a problem.

It took me almost ten years before I was exhausted, trying to keep up the whole house and yard. This exhaustion, along with the emotional surrender work finally got me to accept the fact that I don't "have to have" this house. We could downsize and not have a mortgage. Today I could accept it, and there are things that would even be nice about it. I didn't have to get rid of my house to prove I had surrendered from "having to have it." I simply needed to do the work to emotionally surrender it. I knew I had fully surrendered when I was okay if we lived here or not.

Another example is surrendering to your children growing up. It is the natural and inevitable process. Yet millions of parents struggle with tremendous pain while trying to accept it. Being a mother has fulfilled me tremendously as a person. Yet, I want to encourage my children to fly on their own when it's time. I don't want them to feel held back by me. Recently, I found a Dr.

Seuss quote of the graceful way I hope to be able to do it – "Don't cry because it's over. Smile because it happened." I am thrilled it happened, that I was allowed to be the mother of Mia, Dante and Lexi. I will cherish my new relationship with them as adults. I'm sure there will be tears, but they will be bittersweet tears of how amazing it has all been.

When I was 27, and married Andre, I believed "and the two shall become one" as well as he was supposed to complete me. By eight years of marriage I realized he couldn't, didn't want to and it wasn't even fair to expect him to. I have a high need for emotional connection. Andre has a low need. When we realized this, he said, "Go ahead and get your emotional needs met however you need to. I can't do it and I don't want it." So I took responsibility to join book clubs, conferences, make friends and do work that fill that need for me.

The point of surrender came with realizing that I am a complete person, married or not. If you depend on one person for your happiness, you are setting yourself up for heartbreak. Again, ego is who tells you happiness lies in another person. I had to feel whole alone. This is a big reason I have kept working and continued my interests. The point of health is feeling okay if he is in my life and feeling okay if he is not in my life. My marriage doesn't determine if I am a decent human being or not. The same surrender of attachment applies to my wedding ring – giving up the social need for the ring on my finger to prove someone loves me. Ring or no ring shouldn't change who I am.

Does it make sense to you that sometimes you actually have to get rid of the attachment, and other times you simply have to do the emotional work to get rid of the attachment? You can tell you have spiritually grown when something that used to bother you no longer does, or you can accept it.

A shift in perspective is called a Holy Instance and I have had many in my personal development over the years. Educators call it a paradigm shift. Oprah Winfrey refers to it as an "AHA moment" or "mind orgasm." That is what happened to me in the opening of this book. Whatever you call it, it is a significant learning experience in your life that changes the way you go about life. It can be very exciting or make you sick to your stomach, depending on what it is you just learned.

One of the things I say almost every morning and also every time I take my five-mile meditative walk is *"Please let me see, hear or realize anything that will help me on my journey today."* That is a big invitation to experience life in all of its forms, from happy, sad, mad, thrilled, perplexed, dumbfounded, and elated. Do you mean that every day?

This chapter about experiencing life could go on forever. But I want to make sure I explain one more thing – how destiny and co-creating your life go together. They seem like polar opposite ideas to many people. Destiny means your life is pre-determined before you even get here and there is nothing you can do to change anything that happens in your lifetime. Co-creating, which includes free will, means you can change, add to and eliminate elements in your lifetime. It doesn't have to be an either/or situation. Destiny means you have to accept your lot in life, and it's too bad if you don't like it. And co-creating doesn't mean there is no destiny. Co-creating implies the two together – destiny and free will.

To get the most out of life, you can create your life with your input and destiny working together to model the life you want. I might have been destined to move to Green Bay to teach for one year where I taught with Andre's sister. Andre and I do have matching birth marks on our left elbows. But if we had not chosen to cooperate or co-create our lives we never would have started dating. Co-creating also works with what you don't like in your life. You can change it, hence alternating destiny.

We are co-creating with destiny all the time whether you realize it or not. Destiny doesn't mean done. Stories of redemption are great examples of that. An addict looks destined for an early death and then at some point rehabilitation works and they completely turn their life around. At your high school reunion, people talk about where they thought someone would end up and sometimes they are right and sometimes they are completely wrong.

What do you wish would happen in your life? How proactive are you being about that? Do you care enough to put in some effort? Are you appreciating and caring for the people and things that are going well? One thing is completely true: you are responsible for the experience or art you make of your life. It is a totally different experience if you approach it like you're making an everlasting masterpiece.

Lesson 6
Make it a Great Day!

Do you realize the second you wake up in the morning that you won the lottery of life? You were given one more shot at life, and at that exact time thousands of other people were not as fortunate to wake up? Do you ever think about how lucky you are the second you wake up? You should. What we have taken for granted for years is actually winning the lottery of life. We have been able to do it, day after day, for so long we've lost the wonder and appreciation for it.

When death shows up and we beg for more time, death doesn't understand our plea. Its response is, "I gave you 525,600 minutes last year alone, 24 hours just yesterday and 16, 425 days to date. Now you want to get serious? I'm supposed to believe if you just got a little more time you'd take it seriously and get the most out of it even though you haven't yet? Why should I believe you now? You don't have a good track record."

What would you have to say for yourself? I hope, like me, you'd have one heck of a case to prove you've been Living a Passionate Life! Now can you see how fortunate you are each time you wake up and have the chance to live one more day? We should all be grateful for that. How we can say thank you for one more day is carpe diem, or what I call *Make it a Great Day!*

Our Creator wants us to become our best selves, just as we want the same thing for our children. We can do that one day at a time. Putting ourselves through a range of motion that includes, easy, happy, challenged, peaceful, blissful in order to strengthen the muscle of our character and our lives to where we want to be. Character, as you know, is not built in one day and you can't buy it. You have to earn it. If we approach life like this day is all we have, so we have to give it our all, it will happen. The amazing thing when you approach each day like that is the impact it has over time.

What you are also doing each day is being brave enough to let everyone see who you really are. Socially, we feel comfortable letting others see our character, or even deeper, who we are, when we know they will be accepting. We often feel vulnerable and like to hide if we think people won't like something about us. Yet, to not be able to stand up and say this is who I am, no matter who you are with or what is going on robs you. It actually takes courage to feel vulnerable and stay committed to yourself and the gift of a day that belongs to you.

What constitutes a great day for you? If you are responsible to *Make it a Great Day!* you'll need to know incredibly clearly what that is. Perhaps you want to define your great day by actual specific tasks, or maybe just feelings, or perhaps separately defining great personal days and great professional days. Have you ever thought about starting the day with a clear description on a note card or electronic device and using it as a challenge to go do – EVERY DAY? People *Living a Passionate Life!* do. Your description of a great day may evolve over your lifetime and that's beautiful too. Simply update your description periodically.

What would your description of a great day look like? It is a gift to yourself to define it, and an even greater gift to attempt it. If you're not sure where to start, just use a standard T chart. Draw a line across a piece of paper about two inches from the top and then draw another line from that line down the middle of the page. On the top of the "T," write *Make it a Great Day!* Then on the left side list things that make a great day for you and on the right side list things that ruin your day. After you have this completed, it should give some good insight as to what would make a great day and what you want to keep out of your day. Use this chart to write your great day description. Do I really have to tell you to accept this assignment? Come on, define your great day.

Currently, mine looks something like this – Awaken, fully rested, with gratitude for the profound chance of an amazing day to connect with people, love my family, challenge my personal growth, respect my body, feel spiritually aligned, and make a difference for others. That's what *Make it a Great Day!* means to me personally. How I go about that is by being aware of this intention and trying to fulfill it every day. My actual day is full of people, activities, and places, but preferably only those that include my values and priorities that allow my description of my great day to be possible. Do you see how I could use my description every day whether it was a workday or a weekend? My *Make it a Great Day!* is who I am.

What I want to do is share with you a few of the things I have found, as a professional coach, to be very successful in terms of getting focused so you can *Make it a Great Day!* First I'd like to tell you about some boundaries that set the parameters to be able to Make it a Great Day! So this is basically how you are setting up or protecting your day so you can be proactive in having a great day.

A commitment to having an abundant mentality is a foundational boundary. An abundant mentality is one of the best gifts that you can give yourself and anyone in your life. People who live through an abundant mentality are optimistic, resourceful, supportive, not threatened by other's success, and live from a place of gratitude.

Scarcity mentality, on the other hand, creates negativity, competition, jealousy, judgment, complaining and a constant feeling of lacking something. People who operate from a scarcity mentality are generally not as satisfied with their life as abundant thinkers. When you have an abundant mentality you are not coming from fear, lack or negativity.

Your gifts and talents are completely abundant and meant to be shared freely. You will never run out. If more people understood this concept, the world would be a much happier place. Do yourself a favor and use your gifts and talents.

We are so incredibly fortunate when we live in a free country. We have freedom of choice. That alone can give you an abundant mentality. *Make it a Great Day!* would never come from a poverty mentality. Abundant mentality would tell you that you always have choices. The game is never over until you quit trying.

You need to require more of yourself. That shouldn't surprise you. People having a great day every day aren't just super high on optimism, floating through anything realistic. They might be what you call a master at it. A master makes things look easy, even when it's not. Requiring more of yourself means having a high standard for yourself. You will need to be much more accountable for your time, effort and money. You will have to make sure you are not self-sabotaging, that you are reaching out for support when you need it and that you are using all of your resources. When you require more of yourself you track your schedule, production, results, and finances. Raising the bar is critical to your success at *Making it a Great Day!*

Use your energy for good. Most people don't think of their energy the same way as money. Hopefully, you think before you spend money so that you can make a good decision. Financially, we decide how we are going to save, spend and invest our money. We save money when we want to conserve it and have it for a later date for something we want more than using it right now. We expend money for the things that are worth letting it go for. And we put in money (invest) for the bigger idea that matters to us.

Your energy needs to be thought of the same way. Before you blow it, think – *Do I want to spend my energy on this?* When people are fighting at the store, do you want to spend your energy and get involved? Remember in the last chapter, I referred to it as deciding if you want to lean in (get involved) or lean back (don't get involved). Do you want to use your energy for this (whatever this is)? Using your energy is just like spending your money. And the bigger picture is this: what do you want to invest your energy in? Investing takes a ton of energy. You invest in your passions already. What else do you want to invest your life in?

When you have a boundary around your energy, you use it for good. You don't live by default and throw your energy all over the place each day. You are very clear about what gets your energy and what doesn't. And this may cause you trouble. Don't be surprised if people in your life don't like it if you won't engage with them how you have in the past. Your job is to let it go – don't even try to defend it. We are not responsible to make sure everyone understands our decisions as to how we spend our energy. Do you defend your money decisions to everyone? Energy is the same type of resource. An easy way to decide what gets your energy is your values. A boundary around your energy for your values is a clear boundary. Anything outside your values isn't using your energy for good.

Fear and negativity have to stay outside your boundary because they are toxic. All of us feel fear. Every single one of us has fear – famous or not, young or old. The biggest difference between people who are successful and those who are not is the successful one push through their fear. They feel that fear and they do it anyway. So get the idea in your head that any amount of fear or negativity is toxic to you and you don't want it in your life. Are you going to deal with it rather than allow it to keep you stuck?

So what you want to do is learn some coping skills around fear and absolutely stop the negativity. Just don't participate. Around fear, you want to get used to asking "What's the worst thing that could happen?" I'm sure you're not going to die. I get it that whatever scares you seems enormous at the time you face it down and want to take it on. I have a long list of things I would have sworn were going to kill me and I'm still here writing about it. The point is, if you have this conversation about your fear, you can probably talk yourself down from the drama in your head.

You: *What's the worst that can happen?* Fear: *I'll die.* You: *Is that really going to happen?* Fear: *No.* You: *So what's the worst that can happen?* Fear: *No one will ever speak to me again.* You: *Is that really going to happen?* Fear: *No.* You: *So what's the worst that can happen?* Fear: *I'll feel embarrassed.* You: *Have you ever died of embarrassment before?* Fear: *No, but I don't like it.* You: *Is it worth a little embarrassment if you could (whatever you'll gain by doing the thing you're afraid of)?* Fear: *Yes.* You get the point.

Now you have these great boundaries set for yourself. You're going to have an abundant mentality, you're going to require more of yourself, you're going to carefully decide what you want to do with your energy, and you're going to understand that fear and negativity are toxic.

So now we are going to move on to one of the best things I ever discovered as a professional coach, and that is what I call success habits. Every single person who is living an extraordinary life and is part of the *Make it a Great Day!* club, whether that be with material things or simplicity, has certain success habits that they live by. The success habits are not exactly the same for each member, but every member has them. Because our lives, situations, stages in life and preferences are different, each member will have to create custom success habits for their own life to some extent, but I can give you some general habits that will serve as ideas to get you started.

The first success habit that I have is the concept of *Make it a Great Day!* That is an absolute motto that I live by, and my connotation on "make it" instead of what most other people say, "Have a great day," is that "Have a great day" is passive. "Make a Great Day!" implies it is a choice, and I do that on purpose because I want people to pay attention to the fact that it is a choice. Your day didn't happen to you. You made a decision – how to react to things, how you handled your day, if you were productive or not. So one of my success habits is to *Make it a Great Day!* every day.

So I do conscious things throughout the day to make sure that happens. With children and a husband at home, I started a simple rule that I expect everyone to follow and that is – to have a pleasant good morning. That means no one in my family can be ugly in the morning. You might be saying, "Great Sofia, you're a morning person, but my family isn't." I am a morning person, but my husband is not. When I started this, he was not excited about it. It took months to get him and our three small children on this game plan. But when they saw I wasn't budging on this rule they joined me. They don't have to be talkative and cheery. Minimally, they have to be respectful and allow everyone to start their day in a positive manner.

Too many people start their day as pessimists – "Grrrr! I have to go to work today." "You left your socks on the stairs." "Pick up that wet towel or I'll put it in your bed." "Grrrr!" Ugly, ugly, and more ugly. Stop. If you need to do that, do it in your head or away from your housemates.

Here's why I became such an advocate of this success habit. The way you start your day sets the tone for your whole day. If we started off fighting, crabby, annoyed at each other, that doesn't go away when we leave the house. You know it follows you wherever you are going and continues well into your day. Statistics support this fact and how much your productivity goes down. If you don't believe me, just pay attention yourself for one week. The people who start the day off in toxic negativity, feeling disorganized, and generally yucky don't have as pleasant of a day.

Maybe your pleasant good morning is that you don't want to talk to anyone. You want to be left alone, shower, have your coffee, read the paper and go to work. Fine. Just communicate that to the people who need to know. How your day goes is totally up to you, and you can build that on this concept of *Make it a Great Day!*

We have been on this rule for more than a decade and I can tell you Andre and I are both successful at work, our children get good grades, and it has added to our quality of life. They see the benefit or they wouldn't be cooperating.

Another success habit is to keep doing what you were doing when you were successful. Take out a piece of paper and write at the top "What I am doing when I'm successful." We are trying to evaluate your habits. What is working in your life? When you're at your ideal weight, what are you eating, doing and not doing? When you are successful at work, what are the exact things that lead to that success? When your relationships are at their best, what are you doing to make that happen? When you feel the best about yourself, what is going on? Success leaves clues, and you know yourself the best.

After you're done, take a look at your list from an observation perspective. Are you still doing the majority of the things on your list? Did you forget about some of the things that were working and let them fall to the wayside? My guess is eating ice cream on the couch in the middle of a Wednesday is not on the list. Identify the things you are doing that are not on the list and are not success habits. If you want to be successful in your life (whatever that is to you), you are going to have to do the items on the list you just created.

Another success habit is to keep a schedule. I'm naturally one of the most impulsive, fly-by-the-seat-of-my-pants people you will ever meet. I absolutely love getting into a deep conversation, then start a new project, do something with my children, and then find myself outside in nature wondering what I was doing when I started. However, I know as an adult, with any kind of a maturity level I have to have a scheduled day to some extent for my day to be productive. Time blocking works for me to require more of myself to be successful. My mornings are writing and my afternoons are real estate or I block by the day where Monday/Wednesday/Friday are real estate and Tuesday/Thursday are writing. I don't sit down at 9 a.m. and decide what am I doing to today to *Make it a Great Day!*

A key component of "keep a schedule" is planning your schedule ahead of time. Don't waste your energy arguing about this. Planning your day the night before

Lesson 6 – Make it a Great Day!

and planning your week on Sunday night sets you up for a significantly higher quality of life. I work out of our home which has interruptions and I'm a flitter (research proves it wastes approximately twenty minutes to get back into the task when you come back to it) so I got in the habit of writing a Post-It note defining where I left off. At the end of the day I make myself a brief list of what has to get done the next day, and Sunday night I spend up to thirty minutes planning out my week. Those things alone have massively raised my efficiency.

Keep a schedule takes discipline until it becomes a habit. Boy, I like to do the fun thing first. I use to leave the hardest task until the very end. But over the last ten years in real estate, by keeping a schedule, I have learned to do the tough stuff first and reward myself with fun.

Productivity-wise, a person can get about six things done in a day. Do you know how many items are typically on a person's to-do list? 22. So most people start their days off with an impossible expectation and can't understand why they aren't having great days. An insurance company studied this and reported that 77% of people left work each day feeling bad about themselves as a human being because they couldn't accomplish their to-do list. So as a professional coach I would like to tell you to schedule your top three, but no more than six absolutely-have-to-get-done-or-you'll-die items and see if you can *Make it a Great Day!*

Keeping a schedule is all about how it works best for you. The world of work is even starting to understand we don't all work the same way, just as all students don't learn the same way. So my system and my schedule might not be good for you. I'm just saying get in the success habit of requiring more of yourself by keeping a schedule every day.

Along the same line is tracking your time. Be very conscious of the amount of time you are using and for what during the day. One of the biggest lies workers tell themselves is "Oh, I'm busy. I'm so busy." One of the best success questions I can give you as a coach is "Are you productive or just busy?" There is a huge difference between the two. I don't doubt you are busy. But are you productive? The majority of people are busy: busy sending e-mails, busy making lists, busy running around, busy meeting people, busy, busy, and tired. But what are you producing? The only way to tell if you are productive or just busy is to constantly focus on your results. I would much rather be productive than busy.

One way to focus on productivity is to track by numbers. For example, record the number of sales calls or meeting with a slash, and then record how many resulted in a sale. The second number is the only number that matters because your tracking success, not energy spent. My daughter Mia plays softball and the scoreboard doesn't care how many balls she missed, it only counts the balls she catches to cause a player to be out. I love to meet people. I enjoy coffee dates. But here's where I'll use my success habits and let the person know I'd love to meet with you and I have a half hour. In recent years, I really limit my coffee time for a potential real estate client or a writing friend. That might sound rude, but it's my life and impact matters to me. During the work week I need to be productive more than social. So track your time and answer the question, "Are you busy or productive?" Busy you can tell in your paycheck, and productive you can tell in

Lesson 6 – Make it a Great Day!

your paycheck too.

Another success habit is what I call sacred time. Every single person who has a full life of other people, responsibilities, juggling various challenges, etc. needs to have a system to take care of herself. So by sacred time I mean whatever energizes you. Whatever it is that gets the stress out. I'm an avid reader, and one of my scared times is 4 a.m. or 5 a.m. before anyone but the dogs are up. I make a wonderful pot of coffee, turn the fireplace on in the winter or sit outside in the summer and read for an hour or two. I don't feel guilty because I'm not taking time away from anybody. My creative ideas flow to me during that time, and I often get an answer to something I was trying to figure out. So my sacred time is critical to my pleasant good morning and Make it a Great Day!

Other sacred time for me is writing, my five-mile walk, and time with my family. Yours might be entertainment, sleeping, a hobby, a sport. The things that don't qualify for the concept of sacred time are escapes like drugs, alcohol, gambling, etc. Exercise for your health is a sacred time. It's not about vanity, it's about optimal brain and body functioning. It's sacred not because you love it, but because you have to protect exercise for the extreme benefit it provides to your life. It gets toxins out of your body and primes your brain.

Professionally, sacred time is the crucial success tools you have in order to be successful which might be attending conferences, finding motivational resources, or blowing off steam in a healthy manner. Personally and professionally, sacred time is very much a part of *Make it a Great Day!*

The last success habit I'm going to talk about in

terms of your mindset to *Make it a Great Day!* Is "Watch Your Environment." You may not even realize how much your environment affects your psychology. That doesn't mean everything needs to be neat and pristine all the time. It means noticing what works for you in your environment. Andre prefers neat and clean for his environment. Neat and clean doesn't usually work for highly creative people like myself. I'm visual, and for the longest time I believed if I can't see it (as in papers and projects), I'll forget about it. Things visually stimulate me. I like our dogs, Fiesta and Jose, around me when I work. Andre wouldn't appreciate them at work.

There is one place Andre and I meet perfectly, and that is our custom-built home. We both hate winter. I would be happy to have groceries delivered and stay home for three months, so sunlight was very important to us when we designed and set our house on our lot. The exact little tweaks in our home (environment) have a lot to do with my success. Perhaps no one can tell our house is tilted 12 degrees with full southern exposure, and over 40 windows to get the most light all day long. People can tell our house is set back from our neighbors far enough that we have no view into our house from the street, and woods in the back for privacy. Our entire lot was tree-lined ten years ago and today we enjoy beautiful nature as a privacy fence. I jokingly have called our front porch, where I like to write, my Million Dollar Office because I can see amazing nature for miles that puts me in the most thrilling mood. Our home is full of color and warmth because my family likes it. Our home is an intense example of how important it can be to "watch your environment."

How do you like your environment to be in order for you to have a great day? Quiet, loud, visually calm or busy, temperature, air, cluttered, uncluttered, ergonomic, etc. – all contribute to your environment. Obviously we can't have our environment the way we like it all the time due to work and living with others. But when you can choose, what do you say? I prefer variety and know exactly which environment I need to be in depending on what I'm doing. That's just an example of being very self aware. How do you like to sleep? The environment in your bedroom is critical to induce sleep. A brightly colored bedroom will keep you up at night. Messy bedrooms full of clutter cause bad dreams and are the main reason you don't want your office in your bedroom. Are your environments working for you, or do you need to shape them up a bit to *Make it a Great Day!*?

You don't have to have a lot of money or time to really start paying attention to your environment. Cleaning is free. Brainstorming what can you do to change your environment often comes up with better ideas than if you throw money at it. I started my professional coaching business with a portable file box I worked out of next to the sliding glass door in our old family room. The most common thing you can do to improve your environments is to be aware of how they affect you. Once you know that, you can make a simple plan to improve them. Simplifying your environments is the most popular way people can improve their environment to a level of only having what you love in your spaces.

Now I'm going to give you a few tips for *Make it a Great Day!* **Set the tone for the day.** So beyond the pleasant morning concept, make sure your attitude is ready for the day by showering, checking your intention, being prepared, and deciding you are going for it no matter what that means that particular day. **Get out there.** Life doesn't happen on the couch, so be brave and put yourself in positions that support you in having a great day. **Take a break.** Employers require breaks throughout the day because they are a good idea. Take them in your personal life as well. **Design your ideal life.** That description will allow you to know what you need to do each day to have that. **Don't wait until tomorrow to start over.** Get in the habit of immediately starting over, no matter how many times in a day you have to do that. **Do it now.** Anything that takes less than two minutes you should do now, rather than putting it on a to-do list. And most importantly, **focus on relationships** throughout your day.

If you are going to *Make it a Great Day!* you are going to need some encouragement every once in a while. **Have something to look forward to.** If I'm able to ... or when I'm done... I will see Bryan Weber in my trip example last chapter. Your thing to look forward to might be a break, food, experience, etc. If you'd look forward to it, it should do the trick of getting you through. **Have fun – make a game of it.** Everything in life doesn't need to be hard to achieve it. Learn to make the challenge a game with rewards along the way so you can have fun getting it done. For one thing, it just helps your attitude when you make it a game or have fun. **Join/make a success group.** The point of the group is to challenge, support and propel you forward to reach your goals. It is not a feel-good support group. It is an action group who will call you on your junk when you aren't succeeding. The years that I have participated in a success group I have done so much better on accountability, finances and happiness. **Give yourself permission to say no.** Saying no is a success tip you can choose if it doesn't support your values and goals.

Do I have bad days? Yes, of course, but tremendously fewer than I used to. On a less than stellar day, I try to hang on to as many parts of my great day description as I can, so the whole day is never a loss. If I'm losing the battle I scream "Serenity Now!" and laugh or let the tears come. I know those days are the heavy weightlifting we all have to do. A little self care and a good night's sleep usually make it all go away. The tough days let me know what I still need to work on. Sometimes they let me see a feeling I want to avoid. And sometimes they are warning me about something that needs attention. Every day is valuable.

One of the first things you need to learn during challenges in life is how to bounce, as in bounce back. Resiliency is an incredibly important life skill. The faster and better you can bounce back after losing, failing, or receiving one of life's blows the more you are going to get out of life because you aren't wasting it sitting on the bench of life, devastated. That means you have to deal with the facts and get up and moving again. That means no crying about how it's so unfair. Life has never been fair, and we all have to deal with it. This doesn't mean you can't have an emotional reaction if the situation warrants one. But to have the same emotional reaction over and over again because of the same issue is just staying stuck. Resiliency allows you to have a quick emotional reaction and then ask "Now what?" – as in "Now what do I do?" The focus is on action, and not being a victim. Make a decision that you are going to learn how to bounce, be more resilient, and spend less time sitting out of the game of life.

The average person is just not willing to do what it takes to succeed in life. That's a fact. When you look around and see who appears to be living an extraordinary life, it's a minority. If you choose to *Make it a Great Day!* every day, just know you may be the only one in your house choosing that, or the only one in your office, or the only one at family reunions. If you choose to *Make it a Great Day!* you will be an exceptional person because you are going to go above and beyond what the average person will do.

The most important part of resiliency is to condition your mind. There are still people winning, no matter what the economy is doing. There are people happily married at every stage of the commitment. There are wonderful teenagers. There are people living passionately. Life is good. Great sleep is possible. Older people can be in great shape. We don't have to be polite and listen to pessimism. It's not our fault if we're winning and others aren't. We don't do average and below, or certainly do them any favors by joining them. High expectations do produce results. Under Armour says *"Protect this House,"* I say *"Protect this mind."*

Two options you can use are "putting horse blinders on" or "work like you're going up a mountain." Obviously, you work harder when you are going up a mountain. Going down the mountain is when your life is easy, everything's going your way, and you're lovin' life. However, when do you grow? You grow the most when you're walking up the mountain. So during challenges you are walking up a mountain and, I can guarantee you, you are getting stronger, and forming better success habits to endure the walk – no matter how long or short it will be. People climb mountains every day. So if you can just accept that and decide you are going to bounce back, you will be ahead of the game.

How do you know when it's time to quit? The answer is when you can stomach quitting. How would you feel if you found out you quit just one day away from fulfilling/achieving your God-given purpose? Could you accept it? Would you be sick to your stomach? Would you be begging for another chance? If this could happen and you would be fine with it then you can quit. If you could walk away and have no regrets, you can quit. Quitting is a huge decision. I can't stomach it, so I get in the game every day. If I'm still breathing, I know I'm not done. My faith is tested and I continue believing because I also know I have succeeded many times just because I didn't quit.

Do you know if life was easy we wouldn't get much out of it? Did you realize if life was easy we wouldn't have to help each other, which is one of the main reasons we are here? Some people are able to get important lessons in the joy they experience, but most of us, sadly, don't learn until we feel the pain. Pain gets our attention. Pain tends to get bigger and louder until we address it. And the lessons we learn through pain tend to stay with us longer.

But you know what's exhilarating? Playing all out with everything you've got to the point where you feel strong, exhausted, light-hearted, and joyous about triumphing over the dream or mountain you tackled. Followed up by amazing gratitude for this great ride you just took. In order to live a passionate life, we must dare to show up every day and allow ourselves to truly be seen in a full range of being human. When you are victorious, be humble, and when you feel vulnerable, hold still. For all of it is worth it in the end. That is what *Make it a Great Day!* is all about.

There are two secret weapons that I need to remind you that you already have when it comes to *Making it a Great Day!* The first is your passion. Passion is rocket fuel for the life you want to live. If you're not completely feeling it, look around and see what can be your visual reminders as you go through your day. Pictures, music, quotes, goals, affirmations, intentions, etc. that represent your passion will help you remember your big WHY throughout the day. Your big WHY is your purpose that you're passionate about. When you have an ugly moment, look to your reminders to help you stick it out.

The other secret weapon every person has that will not cost a thing, even if you use it every hour of every day, is perception. You decide how you perceive every fact, story, interaction, opportunity, and situation that comes into your life. The way you perceive things has a huge amount to do with how fulfilling your day is. You can use the secret weapon of perception to realize it's not personal that the other person you encountered took their frustration out on you. That means I see what's happening. I understand the details and dynamics here. I'll own my part, but understanding "you just had a temper tantrum on me" allows you to not interrupt your day over their BS.

The people who are able to manage their perception have a whole lot less stress in their day and are a ton happier. They can feel abundant no matter what amount is in their bank account, because they know gratitude is the greatest abundance there is. Take a look at your perception and see how it could help *Make it a Great Day!*

Lesson 6 – Make it a Great Day!

Finally, you will have to take leaps of faith. There are plenty of times in life when all the facts, figures and resources can't give you the answer. Science can't always prove what's happening. There are no absolute guarantees in life. We have to take risks sometimes. Leaps of faith are falling in love, deciding to have a child, leaving a great career for a newfound passion, following your intuition, or bringing a puppy home when you only meant to go out for a cup of coffee. Life presents a necessity for leaps of faith every once in a while. Which one to choose, this college or that college? You can collect data, feedback, results but in the end, it takes a leap of faith.

When there is nothing else you can do, because you've exhausted all other desperate measures, you find yourself facing a leap of faith. Some people choose white knuckle leaps of faith. Meaning they tense up, hold their breath, close their eyes and just pray it will be over soon. Others are much more skilled at the leap of faith. They are completely relaxed as they absolutely know whatever is going to happen is for their greater good, even if it's ugly at first. They surrender into a leap of faith beautifully and unattached to the outcome. Those are the masters at leaps of faith.

As I have shared earlier, this book itself has been a leap of faith. It started from the moment at The Homestead with the idea and some concepts flowing to me. Each chapter was started without an outline. I'd just relax and put my hands on the keyboard or tape Notes on my iPhone, and let whatever came out be what I needed to say. Several times as I'd realize things, or events in life happened, it would shift the book off in a totally different direction and it would take a bit to figure out what to do with it. At one point it was very uncomfortable because it was getting too "woowoo" for my halfway point between business and personal writing. I had to keep my commitment to just go with it and let the book lead me. I hadn't really talked about God, spirituality, or parenting publically before. It made me feel vulnerable and too exposed. When it kept showing up and wouldn't go away, I knew it had to be included.

What makes taking a leap of faith even more intimidating is other people thinking we're nuts for taking them. It's hard when we don't completely understand leaps of faith ourselves, except that we feel incredibly drawn to do it. When you find yourself in that position, it is a sacred lesson. You have to believe in yourself in order to take a leap no one else understands. It is in those leaps that we realize we can believe in ourselves.

When I got within three weeks of finishing this book, I just felt like I needed to go to Mexico, by myself, to do my final edits. I have been to Mexico several times before and know what the environment is like, and it was calling me. There is something to be said about removing yourself from your life and being alone thousands of miles away in a very different, beautiful, culture with your thoughts. Just like my California trip last spring, it changes you with all your senses when you put yourself in a completely different environment. Julia Cameron, author and writing teacher, calls them "artist dates." I wanted an artist date with myself and this manuscript in Mexico. I told Andre I was going, I didn't ask permission. I heard a few comments from people concerned about me going to Mexico on my own. I was undeterred, as I was taking a leap of faith: The act of believing in or accepting something intangible or

Lesson 6 – Make it a Great Day!

unprovable, or without empirical evidence.

There are leaps of faith that are absolutely stupid, of course, but, if they are not ours, who are we to say? The only one we get to judge is looking back at us in the mirror.

There won't be a parting of the seas, or a miracle dream sequence, when you decide to take leaps of faith. They may begin simply when you decide to take them, mark them on your calendar or state "I'm doing this." No matter what leaps of faith begin with you putting energy out into the universe signaly you are ready to take the leap. You might be a public or a private leap-taker. Some people feel stronger about the leap if they make it public, because they know everyone is watching them and it's harder to back down. Maybe that's part of weddings with a crowd. Others prefer to be quiet until the leap worked out so they can look like they knew what they were doing.

Every once in a while I can hear my children saying "YOLO" – You Only Live Once. That's the teenage infallibility I miss as an adult. The parent in me wants to warn, "That's fine as long as you're not talking about risky behavior with a car." But then I soften, because what they are talking about is Dante trying to convince Mia they should go "coning." Coning is when you order an ice cream cone from a drive through and when you get to the window you grab only the ice cream and drive off, leaving the confused employee holding the cone. To my knowledge they have never done this but, they sure like to laugh about the idea of doing it.

They are right about the message of YOLO. YOLO belongs in every day. So given everything we have talked about that goes into *Make it a Great Day!*, what are you inspired to put into your day? What do you want to take out? What are your success habits, tips, and boundaries? How's your perception? I'm sure you have never thought this much about what goes into a fabulous day and I hope you do going forward. I use *Make it a Great Day!* as my salutation to remind myself and pass the message to others. Feel free to join me if it moves you.

Lesson 7
Passion Workers!

I'm a passion worker. I have always been a passion worker. Can you say you are a passion worker, to anyone, with great confidence? Don't worry. You won't get arrested for it. Mother Teresa, Bill Gates, Blake Mycoskie, Mattie Stepanek, Oprah Winfrey, Pearl Fryar, Carol Mooney, Beto Perez, Georgia O'Keeffe, Rosa Parks, and Dr. Mehmet Oz are all passion workers and happy to say so.

Passion workers are people who are passionate for the work they do or a cause. They can be found in for-profit and non-profit work. Even if they get a paycheck, they would do the work for free. Those are the people who are often envied by onlookers for finding their bliss and getting paid for it – hence, winning the career lottery. The passion for a cause includes charities as well as promoting topics like justice, saving the earth, mental health, youth athletics, gender equality, privacy rights, politics or the like. Passion workers feel incredibly drawn to their work or cause and have great internal motivation to do the work, often for intrinsic rewards, and without prodding from others.

Passion workers are respected and sometimes coveted, for they have found the deep purpose others yearn for. They aren't the ones going from job to job, unsatisfied and seeking. They are the ones who leave or move only when it gets them closer or deeper into their passion. When they are honoring their calling they feel fully alive, motivated, stimulated and exhilarated. Who wouldn't want that? Fulfillment is what people see and what they would like for themselves. Passion workers are equally giving as much as they're getting. The passion worker and the work or cause gives each other energy to keep going.

What people don't always realize is that it may be the work they do or what they do outside of work. Andre is evaluated as outstanding at his job, but he goes to his passion – youth athletics – after work. The years I was not happy with my work were the years I was confused by this. Not everybody earns a paycheck from their passion, and some people don't even want to co-mingle money and passion. Other people have found their passion, but they can't make it pay the bills. When I realized I do one thing to pay the bills that allow me to have my passions, I looked at my job differently. I quit expecting it to make me feel passionate. The way I do my businesses allow me to be around my family the most, and my family is my first passion.

Writing Sofia Michaels books is a passion that I no longer give any commercial expectations. My commitment when I write is that it is enough for me to have the cathartic journey and place each book on my bookshelf as a scrapbook of my life. If they help others or have commercial appeal it is a bonus. And whether my children care or don't care, I have captured my essence on the page for when I am no longer physically here. Always the eternal teacher, sorry, but it's the mother in me.

I started writing in 2007, and it didn't start out as passion. My first book was written in my legal name as a how-to book for entrepreneurs, and I did have commercial expectations for it. I listened to the wrong mentor, Janet Switzer of Jack Canfield fame, and turned the book into an expensive at-home training course with audio CDs. After doing that, I realized you have to get into the whole online sales business, which, as you heard about in lesson six, is a business I don't want to be in. This experience wasn't passion for me, and in hindsight I didn't even like it.

Why didn't I quit writing? There was one reason – my intuition. Something about writing kept calling me. My original writing attempt came from the advice that many sources give, which is to write about what you know. Well, I was a Masters-level educator of marketing and personal branding. So a how-to book on that subject seemed obvious. What I didn't take into account was that I was changing a lot as a person. This idea of writing about my life kept coming to my mind. I rejected it for quite awhile because I had never taken a writing class before. I certainly was no English major. And who in their right mind would just start writing about their life with no fan base or request for it?

My first Sofia Michaels book was not passion either. It was a tool to save my emotional life. It was the last thing I wanted to do, so I knew it was a last attempt effort I had to take. The four months of writing it were the most painful and cathartic experience I have ever had to date. I was physically and emotionally sick the whole time as I puked out each chapter. By the time I wrote the last words, I had a new awe of and respect for the writing process.

Then I was ready to use writing to get to the life I wanted. It was not until my fourth book, the second Sofia Michaels book, that passion grabbed me. I had found a way of writing scrapbooks of my life that inspire myself and others, that I had fallen deep in love with. In the end, my writing passion became an artistic style that completes me as self-expression of living.

The struggle to find your voice is a common life struggle. Usually that "voice" is not literally a speaking, writing or singing voice. It refers to self-expression without fear of retaliation. It also refers to stating, with confidence and conviction, this is who I am. Most people would do that with everyday actions, comments, decisions, etc. Finding your voice can be hard if family, a spouse or co-workers don't want you to. Remember deathbed regret number one? "I wish I'd had the courage to live a life true to myself, not the life others expect of me."

Specifically and personally, Andre and our children have always been surprisingly supportive of my Sofia Michaels writing. Andre was the biggest surprise, as he saw first-hand how much this cathartic writing helped me and how much I enjoy it. He also knows I have always held myself to a very high integrity level to not write out of anger. The writing is processed through my mind, reflected on and edited, which happens over months. Anger is really pain being masked anyway. Above all, he knows the writing is from my perspective as a human being that encompasses my entire experiences to date.

I had a habit of constantly checking with him, out of insecurity, on each book or topic. "Are you sure you don't want to read it first, in case you aren't fine with it?" Which I realize is not integrity in writing, but the health of my marriage trumps that as I can omit any details he wouldn't want included. My greatest respect for Andre comes in his final comment, "I accepted a long time ago that my wife is an author. You can stop asking me. I'm sure." I still get the urge to check with him, but out of respect for what he said, I make myself refrain.

The person who keeps challenging me about using my voice is Mia, our 16-year-old. If she ever hears me say, "I want to write about X, but I'm not sure (it's safe)" or "I want to say it like X, but that might be too much for some people." Mia says one of two things she has learned from me 1) Our favorite quote by Marianne Williamson about not shrinking to make others comfortable or 2) "Well-behaved women rarely make history" (a bumper sticker on my office door to remind me to go ahead and say it.) I appreciate Andre and Mia for helping me to be brave when I need it.

So you may not understand my passion for writing about life, mine in particular as the source, but all I can say is that it has become me. It is what I think about each day, look forward to, have a yearning to do, experience a full range of emotions doing, and blissfully enjoy all of the creativity and ideas that make my whole body and mind feel amazing. I can do it all by myself, or involve other people or experiences. I can do it whether I fit in my jeans or am getting more wrinkles. Actually, the more I age the better result, because it is about my spirit experiencing life and not my exterior. I can write in our home, wherever my children are, or on trips. In the grocery store when ideas hit me I can quickly type a note in my iPhone for later. So writing is the tool of my passion, and my purpose comes from one particular thing that just clicked for me and gave me those same goose bumps all over the minute I heard it.

Joel Osteen, pastor of Lakewood Church, gave a sermon about all of the people who have wasted their gifts and took them to the graveyard with them. Who knows if someone in the cemetery could have found the cure for cancer, created world peace, or solved hunger, was his message. I was instantly propelled to do everything I can to inspire people to exhaust their gifts/talents before they die. What propelled me at first was a panic regarding what a waste a graveyard full of talent is. Human potential wasted raises in me a deep need to do something about it. What clicked for me was that I was already aware of my appreciation for my God-given talents, and I knew since 17 years of age that I was using them to show my gratitude to Him, and now I knew what I was missing was I had to inspire others to do the same.

My Personal Reason WHY, or Purpose

God gave me amazing gifts when I was born, and I can show him my gratitude for those gifts by using them to their fullest extent and encouraging everyone I encounter to do the same to constantly improve the world and our experience here.

I was trusted with these gifts because God knew I would use them and am on a very specific journey which has made me well equipped. I wake up every single day feeling motivated to carry out this purpose in a variety of fun and exciting ways.

This purpose and cause was so important to me I dedicated the second act of my life to it. For my *Personally Branded* book cover I even tattooed my slogan "Use Your Talents" on my right shoulder where I was shown from the back in a red cocktail dress in Puerto Rico. My mom, Pillar, said "Couldn't you have used a Sharpie (marker)?" Yes, I could have and maybe I should have. But that's passion. I permanently meant it. Besides, it can be covered up. It's not fatal. It's creativity, a gift from God and my mom.

Regardless of how you went about determining your purpose (born knowing, discover or decide) it will always be a personal spiritual journey. Career counseling looks at your skills and puts you somewhere. My high school aptitude test recommended I become a politician. My spirit said, "Are you crazy? That is the furthest thing from my interests." In hindsight, the people part and the desire to improve society part of being a politician was correct, but the point is, you have to continually check with your spirit as well.

Since you already know what your passions are, I'm going to entertain you by showing you passionate people in different styles of expressing it so that they may inspire you further. Even the same passion is not expressed in the same manner by different people. One of the gifts of mature passion is that you realize it's not your job to make sure people understand your passion. It just matters if the passion is worth spending your one and only life on.

The public story of Steve Jobs is inspirational. I would be the first to say I was impressed with his ability to start a dream from his parents' garage and turn it into a remarkable business that out-lives him.

In my first marketing class in college I learned about Steve Jobs in my textbook. My first personal computer as a student teacher was a Macintosh. I've had an iPhone since the first one came out. I admit, I wanted a piece of his imagination and creativity. What I respected so much is he was a street-smart learner in life, having dropped out of the traditional college path and instead made his own educational experience. He fit the little rebel in me.

After Steve Jobs passed on October 5, 2011, I knew I would read his authorized biography by Walter Isaacson because I wanted to know more about this remarkably passionate man. I had heard Steve Jobs was incredibly private his whole life. Then I heard he wanted Walter to write his memoir so that his kids would understand what he had done when he wasn't around. That made me a little nervous, as I knew he had three kids. One was a daughter he denied was his until she was in her twenties. Was he one of those workaholics who sacrificed everything for a dollar, was he driven by ego, or was it something else? He always had a reputation for being intense and having a sense of urgency, which are certainly traits of passion workers.

The truth is, I wish I hadn't read his biography. He was not the kind of person I would admire, knowing the whole story. The sentence "He was the cruelest Zen person I ever met" is the saddest oxymoron I've ever read. His daughters were harmed the most. I would

Lesson 7 – Passion Workers!

never have worked for him knowing the way he treated employees. But what blew my mind the most is that so many people drank the Steve Jobs Kool-Aid and put up with his treatment. "Those around Jobs referred to his ability to influence the perception of those around him as his 'reality distortion field'."

However, Steve Jobs was a college dropout who turned into a visionary who taught the world to think differently about technology, work, entertainment and life. I have respect for that amazing feat.

Every person gets to decide what is worth their life. For Steve Jobs' business, the way he did it, was worth his lifetime. For me, I'm not willing to spend my life that way. People, particularly my family, matter most to me. But it's not my place to judge. It's how Steve Jobs chose to spend his life. We all get to choose every day of our lives. On the business front he will always have a legacy of innovation, creativity, and fundamentally changing seven industries with the intense passion he gave to those pursuits every day of his life.

Mother Teresa, on the other hand, you could argue was the opposite of Steve Jobs, being compassion for all people above all else. She so passionately followed what she believed to be the word of God that she took a vow of poverty for herself in order to serve the poor, and dedicated her entire life to that pursuit.

I learned something brilliant about Mother Teresa a few years ago that changed my life. She was never AGAINST anything. She was only FOR what she believed in. Mother Teresa knew to be against anything put negative, toxic energy into the world. She did not want to be associated with that. To be against something, even with the best intentions, focuses on negativity and toxic energy and puts more of that into the world. She simply put her energy, words and action TOWARDS what she wanted to achieve in a positive manner. Rather than being against war, she was simply for peace. Rather than complain about what's not working, you would train yourself to focus on *How would I like it to be and how can I make that happen?*

That may seem like an insignificant difference, yet it is not. She was a leader of people, and in order to use her influence for good she needed to bring her followers to where she wanted them to go (peace) and not to stir them up to what they hate (war.)

Today, there are plenty of people who believe you do not have to take on a vow of poverty to serve the Lord and may not see the title of "martyr" as one worth aspiring to, but for Mother Teresa, that was part of her passion and the way she chose to spend her life.

When you believe in passion, part of its beauty is in understanding that you don't get to judge people's passion. My dad loved working on cars. I have no interest in cars. I love public speaking. My mom would rather not speak in front of five people. Yet she can paint amazing pictures and she began painting at 60. We each have a right to chose our passions and even change them over our lifetimes if we like to, even if no one but ourselves understands it.

Mattie Stepanek was a child who delivered his passion to the world. Did you realize children can do that? Passion workers have no age limitations. Mattie left a legacy as a poet and essayist in 13 years that the majority of 90-year-olds never do. Mattie was known as the Heartsong Kid and had Oprah Winfrey, Jimmy Carter, Maya Angelou, Steven Spielberg and countless others wrapped around his finger. They knew he was a prodigy prophet for peace. He even co-authored a book about peace with former President Jimmy Carter.

Mattie's website states his mission – "He wanted people to feel happy – and he wanted to spread peace."

Mattie believed that we are each born with a *"Heartsong"* — or a reason for being and a purpose in life. He shared and celebrated that "Hope is real, peace is possible, and life is worthy!" — if we each choose to embrace such truths in attitude and action, for ourselves and for our world.

Mattie said he wanted to be remembered as *"a poet, a peacemaker, and a philosopher who played."*

Maya Angelou was his role model for writing. "She has a gift for shaping words for others and teaching powerful lessons that take even the most oppressed past into a positive future, filled with opportunity," he said. Can you imagine what a profound impact this child and his writing had to gain Ms. Angelou's private attention? One of Mattie's three wishes was to see Shrek, and it was not released yet. Steven Spielberg actually sent an executive with his own copy of the yet-to-be-released Shrek movie in a briefcase that was handcuffed to her wrist to the hospital for a private showing just for Mattie.

Mattie's mother, Jeni Stepanek, wrote the book *Messenger: The Legacy of Mattie J.T. Stepanek and Heartsongs* after he passed away. I had watched Mattie on Oprah over the years and knew it was a passion book I had to read out of support to him and his mother. As I chose to read the book on a Florida vacation, I had no idea what I was getting myself into. It was incredibly inspiring, and it was also gut-wrenching to read as a mother. As I read his mother's words, I couldn't imagine how she and Mattie soldiered through the death of all four of her children (due to inheriting a rare and fatal neuromuscular disease called Dysautonomic Mitochondrial Myopathy which Jeni, didn't know she carried the gene until she was diagnosed as an adult and faced her own death.) Several times on the plane, tears were dripping from my face as I tried to even fathom that plight in life as a mother. I would have to stop reading for a bit because I couldn't take it anymore. The last three chapters were the hardest reading I have ever done. But the passion of Mattie and Jeni Stepanek moved me deeply.

Anyone would have understood in the face of incredible medical illness and financial challenges resulting from it if they couldn't or didn't want to contribute anything to the world. But that's not what happened. Their illness actually drove them with an urgency to try and deliver as much passion and purpose to the effort of spreading hope and peace before time ran out. Jeni's purpose was to support her son in fulfilling his, and she has gone to extensive heroic effort to do that.

Today Mattie Stepanek has a park and a foundation dedicated to his honor, as well as several of his books that continue to serve his purpose and legacy. We often think it takes longevity to make an impact, and yet we can see in Mattie Stepanek that is simply not true. A big impact in a short amount of time is possible whether it is when you are young, middle-aged or old. Let that inspire you to make an impact today.

Passion workers can be fun in order to have an impact. Steve Irwin, nicknamed "The Crocodile Hunter", was an Australian wildlife expert, television personality, and conservationist who lit up a room when he walked in. Steve had charisma with eyes that twinkled with passion when he was educating the world about crocodiles. It has been said he did more for tourism in Australia than any other source.

Steve Irwin had high energy that you could physically see and hear as he moved in front of the camera. What was interesting was he wore the same khaki shirt and pants when he was working which became the neutral background to showcase his big personality. He was like a small child seeing the magic of Santa on Christmas morning when he talked about his passion.

Steve's father was a wildlife expert interested in herpetology, while his mother Lyn was a wildlife rehabilitator. Steve received his first 12-foot scrub python for his sixth birthday and wrestled his first crocodile at the age of nine. Not exactly a traditional childhood, but one that ignited a passion that became his purpose in life. His entire family was involved in his passion, including Steve's wife Terri and their two children. Part of Steve's legacy was the fact that his was on film. So if you missed out on his passion while he was alive, you can simply Google him now to see videos of this passionate man in action.

It is often the famous examples that get our attention, or even make us feel like we haven't done anything unless it's on a big scale or stage. That's simply not true either. When I have used well-known people as examples in my books, it is purely for the fact that you might know who I'm referring to and therefore get a better understanding of the concepts I'm describing.

Thank goodness there are tons of passion workers who aren't famous by society's standards. There are passion workers all around you. Some will be obvious to you because they externally express their passion, and others you may need to look for and invite to be more open, as they are introverts about their passion. But what is beautiful about observing and interacting with passion workers is that it can fuel your own inspiration.

I met Dr. Carol Mooney when I was seventeen years old and running for Wisconsin State DECA President. As an adult she had made the effort to come introduce herself to me. While I realized she went out of her way to do that, as a teenager, I didn't really understand why she would do that. Dr. Mooney reached out to me several times over the next 18 months, as I had been fortunate to be accepted in the Marketing Education program at University of Wisconsin-Stout, where she taught.

I wasn't a teenager who traditionally makes it to college. In those days I would have been labeled "an at-risk youth" and those teenagers didn't often get a chance nor were they able to make it all the way to a degree very often. If they got the Golden Ticket of admission, they were a large majority of the nationwide 45% freshman dropout/kicked out by the end of first semester.

To tell the truth, I wondered my whole senior year of high school if my acceptance to UW-Stout was orchestrated by Jeff Abbott, my high school marketing teacher, Marie Burbach, my State DECA Advisor, and Dr. Mooney. Other than the fact that I was standing out in marketing and DECA, I didn't understand how I was getting a shot. (Carol, Jeff and Marie, if that was the case, don't ever tell me as that was one of the greatest gifts of my life.)

She wanted to be called Carol by her students, not Mrs. Mooney (she didn't have her doctorate back then.)

Carol became my professional mentor. I had never had professional women, with degrees, in my life before. I watched Carol as she tirelessly gave of herself, exuded passion for marketing education and DECA, connected with students as human beings, and personally guided me to graduation – twice.

She NEVER cancelled class, because it would be cheating the tuition we had paid for an education. Carol carpooled over an hour each way to work, even in treacherous winter storms. If she could make it, we could make it from our housing on campus. Although she never stated this, we just knew it was her expectation, and I thank her for that now.

If you look up the word "professional" in the dictionary, it would reference her name. Above that, ethics and integrity are a strong part of her passion and always have been. She has always complimented me on my integrity when in actuality it came from her effect on me and the injustice I came from. I remember when she told me she was going to complete a doctoral program. I even said something to the effect of, "how are you going to do that with everything you have going on in your life?" Carol replied, "I need to show my students that I am a life-long learner too. I want to take the challenge for myself, and it's good for the university. I'll fit it in." That, right there, is Carol.

When I was finishing my master's degree, also at UW-Stout but years later, I chose Carol as my thesis advisor. At the time, Mia was one year old, and I was in my third trimester of my second pregnancy, taking an educational law class an hour and half away and teaching full time. We never talked about the challenge. I just knew, and she knew I knew, that if she could do it, I could do it. She never would have told me if she had concerns about my ability to finish on time. Professional examples like Carol, for female students in particular, are proof anything is possible. Even though I have never drank grape juice again (written about in *Pretendia*) I did graduate with my master's three weeks before Dante was born.

Carol was a lighthouse for me during those years. No matter what storms I was going through, I knew she would always be there with her ever-present light and strength. One of her talents is inspiring students to believe they can do it on their own. She doesn't interfere, take over, place doubt, try to control the outcome, or dictate anything. Master educators are a "guide on the side" and not just a "sage on the stage." Carol is certainly a master educator.

Carol remains a friend in my life, someone I respect and look up to. We have transitioned beautifully in our relationship from a 17-year-old girl and her college mentor to strong professional women. I cherish the dinners and glasses of wine we have every so often to catch up on each other's lives. Dr. Mooney remains committed to UW-Stout and has been promoted to professor and program director for the graduate degrees in Career and Technical Education where she is making an even bigger impact. It often takes just one person in your life to make a life-changing difference like that. I have been fortunate to have more than one.

A guidance counselor at my son Dante's school had been especially helpful to our family during Dante's 7th grade year. In September, Dante suffered a severe concussion during a football game. We were fortunate to have the University of Wisconsin Badgers football trainer as our pediatrician since our children were born, who is a concussion expert. Dr. Bernhardt said,

"No school, only a dark room, no video games or television besides the History Channel. His brain needs to completely rest in order to heal." To say I was concerned about Dante's brain and his future would be an understatement. Mr. Weitzel, Dante's counselor, told me not to worry about school. But Dante was an A student and in advanced math, so I still worried a little. Mr. Weitzel communicated with all of Dante's teachers for us and got frequent medical updates as we received them.

After two weeks of missed school, Dante was cleared to go back to school after an impact concussion test and, shockingly, was also cleared to play football. He had been back in school not more than a week when, during his first football game back, he suffered another severe concussion. Now I was really worried about his brain. We took him out for the rest of the season and he missed two more weeks of school. Mr. Weitzel was always so calm and able to look at the bigger picture. Dante was even starting to get worried about missing school and his grades. When you have a severe concussion you can't do homework because it stresses the brain. After a total of one month of missed school, Mr. Weitzel promised me he would personally see that Dante was transitioned back into school with all his classes.

Everything was great until Mother's Day.

Dante woke up on Mother's Day 2012 and said, "Mom, my back is really hurting." A few days later an MRI discovered he had broken his back on both sides of his 4th vertebrae. Dante didn't even know how he had done it. Dr. Bernhardt said, "Well, taking hits in football, constantly rebounding in basketball, a 37" vertical jump and clearing five feet on high jump (He was five feet four inches tall) is probably what did it." Until that year, Dante had never been hurt in athletics.

Again, Mr. Weitzel helped coordinate with all his teachers that Dante could have a Pillow Pet for his back, get up and stand whenever he needed to, and be excused from gym class for the rest of the year. I really appreciated everything Mr. Weitzel did for Dante that year. Dante spent 90 days that summer in a full back brace, unable to do anything physical but walk.

In July, we were driving in the car when out the blue Dante said, "Oh yeah, Mom, Mr. Weitzel died kayaking." Those are the kind of sentences that make your mind stop for a minute. You can't fathom what was just said. "What did you say, Dante?" I said in a flat, monotone voice. "Mr. Weitzel was kayaking in June and his kayak tipped over. He couldn't get it to turn back over, and he died," Dante stated. I felt an instant panic of sadness as he was such a good teacher and we lost him. Dante, with the wisdom of a 14-year-old, said, "Mom, he died doing what he loved." At the time, that didn't sit well with me. I was focused on how sad that was for his family, and it is always sad when passion workers disappear from this earth.

Mr. Weitzel and his passion for outdoor recreation stayed on my mind for almost six months before I changed my thinking. For Mr. Weitzel personally, was it sad he died doing his passion rather than any other way? We are all going to die. Perhaps dying doing your passion is a much better way to go out than some pointless way.

One day when we were sitting at a waterpark, I asked Andre about it. "Are you going to have a heart attack at a basketball game someday?" He said, "Yeah, coaching. Coaching somewhere would be good." He

Lesson 7 – Passion Workers!

asked me "And are you going to die writing somewhere?" I answered "Yeah, writing somewhere about Mia, Dante and Lexi."

Even though I didn't want him to, Dante did return to football the following year after being completely cleared by Dr. Bernhardt. Andre was the coach, so it was either World War III in our marriage or I had to come to terms with it. I finally said what any wife or mother shouldn't say: "I am turning my back, and if anything happens to him it is on you and Dr. Bernhardt. I hate this sport." Andre's solution to my discomfort was to move Dante to quarterback instead of running back, because quarterbacks don't run "as much." Well, it was either my stupidity at trusting that idea or Running Chief (Dante) himself, but he racked up 26 running touchdowns in nine games that season.

This is what happens when you're a mom who promotes dreams and passion. My smart children remember things like "You don't get to judge other people's dreams" or "Nothing's impossible. The world itself says I AM POSSIBLE." – Audrey Hepburn. Dante told me I was looking at the game in the wrong way (barbaric). I explained to him my greatest concern was if he got Alzheimer's disease when he was old, and I wouldn't be around to take care of him. With the cutest slight tilt of his head, he questioned me, "Maybe I would have a wife who would take care of me?" And with that sweet heart-felt comment I said, "No matter what happens to you, I pray you will have a spouse who wants to take care of you."

Doubting your passion or being disillusioned by it can be incredibly painful for passion workers. I think it's an incredibly small percentage of people who are born knowing what they are passionate about and that passion continues their entire life without issues. Doubting your passion or being disillusioned by it can be as painful and devastating as an affair in your marriage or a loss of identity.

When Andre and I were in Virginia at The Homestead, the same place as where I opened this book, we were scheduled to take The Cascades Gorge hike with a guide, the CEO of the company Andre works for, and numerous other employees on this reward trip. It was so hot that I had worn a racerback tank top. I was a little self-conscious about the CEO seeing my "Use Your Talents" tattoo on my right shoulder. I didn't want it to affect Andre's career. For the first part of the hike, I stayed behind him. Brian La Fountain was the naturalist who led our group. The minute I laid eyes on him, I knew he was a passion worker. Everyone was talking about the fact that Brian was the best guide and we were so fortunate to be able to have him, as his hikes are always booked. When he opened his mouth I knew he should be on television on some nature or naturalist show promoting the wonderful facts he was sharing in such a gregarious way.

For hours, Brian continued to share his knowledge through the most beautiful waterfalls and trails I had ever seen. At one point there was nothing I could do to remain behind Mr. CEO, as he had stopped over on the side of the trail and wasn't moving. The group started to move and I just decided, "oh, well" and moved on the trail, leaving Mr. CEO behind. The next thing I knew, a hand grabbed my right arm and another one rested on my back just below the base of my neck. Before I could get turned around to see who it was I heard a man's voice say, "What does it say?" As he let go of me and I turned around, it was Brian with a stunned look on his face. I knew something significant was happening for him as I've seen that *aha* face before in coaching sessions. I told him it says "Use Your Talents!" and he said, "I have to tell you something when we finish the hike."

When we reached the end of the trail, Brian grabbed my hand and quickly led me off in an area away from the group where they could still see us but not hear what Brian was saying. He went on to explain to me that he had been having a lot of trouble with his manager and was contemplating quitting, as the criticism from the boss was making him question whether being a trail guide was even what he should be doing. Before he came to work that day he had prayed for a sign to let him know if being a trail guide was really his passion. When he looked up and saw my tattoo, on his trail, he was amazed to see that as a clear sign to him.

"Brian, I am not certain about the specific decision you are trying to make, but I can assure you that what I saw on the trail today was certainly passion. I noticed it right away. There is no question about that" I said. He commented about how thrilled he was that he had gotten that sign and I was supposed to be on his trail today. I knew exactly what he meant. I told him I was writing this book and that the experience was fantastic for me as well. We thanked each other and took a picture together to remember the event.

When I re-joined the group it felt a little awkward, as the senior executives and their wives wanted to know what all of that was about. Andre was used to exuberant people reacting and needing to talk to me, as I have been a professional coach for a long time. Andre just said, "I realized he must have really needed to talk to you." Although the executives and their wives were getting a little concerned about what was going on, Andre was not. I generically explained the situation to them, leaving out the deep spiritual understanding.

Brian's not the only one who questions himself or doubts his passion. Tom Shadyac questioned his passion in a huge way. Tom Shadyac was a multi-millionaire writer and movie director of *Ace Ventura: Pet Detective, Liar Liar, The Nutty Professor, Patch Adams*, and more famous films. After suffering a severe concussion from a bicycle accident that lasted for months, Tom decided to sell his 17,000 square foot mansion in California and moved into a 3,000 square foot trailer that houses his family as well as his entire business with space for staff. He questioned his previous passion for Hollywood, the limelight, materialism, excessive staff and overhead costs.

Did people in his famous/materialistic world think he was crazy to give it all up? Yes. Regardless of what kind of lifestyle you are from, people may think you're crazy to radically change your life unless you are going in the direction of bigger, better, more. Extreme simplicity doesn't register with many. What people didn't understand about Tom's life change was it had nothing to do with materialism. That is what all the stories reported about because it was sensational, but it was actually about Tom questioning the profound experience life is, which has nothing to do with materialism.

While people are in the stage of pain, trying to figure out what's wrong or changing about their passion, it is often referred to as bankruptcy of the soul. There is nothing worse than bankruptcy of the soul for human spirits. On a life satisfaction scale, it doesn't even register as a level one. The process of working through that and figuring out what would make your passion shine again can take months or even years, depending on what you are doing about it.

When bankruptcy of the soul is at its worst, you may experience dark night. Dark night is not actually a new age woo-woo concept. The term "dark night (of the soul)" is used in Christianity for a spiritual crisis in a journey towards union with God, like that described by 16th century Saint John of the Cross in his original poem describing it. For most people, dark night is incredibly painful and easiest to understand by the death of an extremely close loved one, and how you'd be feeling. Sometimes it only lasts a night or two (thank goodness.) The night Elizabeth Gilbert spent on the bathroom floor in *Eat, Pray, Love* was a dark night. The four months of writing my memoir in the winter of 2008 was dark night for me. Tom Shadyac's concussion recovery was dark night. It's so much worse than depression. It's anxiety and self-hate on fire.

Dark night of the soul is like labor and birth. If you live through it, the re-birth of your soul is amazing. Gratitude, clarity, and a new path appear. There is light where everything used to be drastically dark. For Tom Shadyac, the clarity came in a new project (film) and releasing almost all of his societal trappings.

Simplicity and profound questions about life itself became a passion for Tom. He created a documentary entitled *I AM* that asked two questions – "What's wrong with our world, and what can we do about it?" He believes the lie is our external definition of success. For Tom, the lighter he got with his life, the happier he was. Rather than focus on what our culture tells us, he urges everyone to look within themselves for how they want to live. Needing to be significant at the expense of someone else, why do we live like this? – is how Tom's thought process changed. That's a good example of seriously questioning your passions, and also a good example of passions changing over time. He even ended up writing an ebook *Life's Operation Manual* as a result of his experience.

The only difference between where you are and where someone else is the way you think. Skills and ability can be taught. Mindset is really the Golden Ticket to the life you want to live. Mindset, when it comes to Living a Passionate Life!, helps you to reserve your energy for your highest, best use. It helps you reflect: if you are doing something anybody else can do, you're probably missing your purpose and passion.

Mindset helps you keep thinking, "There has to be a better way," which results in passion workers, passionate causes and passionate companies. My choice for Book of the Year in 2011 was *Start Something That Matters* by Blake Mycoskie. I'll tell you where his passion started, but what clicked for me in business was his concept of entrepreneurship, not charity, to raise money for social causes.

It's more than conscious capitalism. Conscious capitalism is about "creating a successful business that also connects support to something that matters to them and that has great impact in the world." TOMS is an entrepreneurial venture created specifically for a social cause. Another *aha* moment for me. Market research today says that given similar products, customers will buy a product that supports a social cause over one that doesn't. That is a consumer shift in the marketplace.

Lesson 7 – Passion Workers!

   Tom and his sister Paige first sprinted through Argentina in 2002 while they were competing on the CBS reality show "The Amazing Race" (as fate would have it, after thirty-one days of racing around the world, they lost the million-dollar prize by just four minutes). In 2006, Tom took some time off from work, as he believes it's critical for his soul to take a vacation no matter how busy he is, and he chose to return to Argentina. On this trip he became aware of how many children didn't have the national shoe, the alpargata, or any shoes to protect their feet and health. There were already some shoe drives, but millions of children were still left barefoot.

   "There has got to be a better way," stayed on Blake's mind until he thought, "Why not come up with a solution that guaranteed a constant flow of shoes, rather than being dependant on kind people making donations?" That is a brilliant thought! When passion struck Blake he decided, "I'm going to start a shoe company that makes a new kind of alpargata. And for every pair I sell, I'm going to give a pair of new shoes to a child in need. There will be no percentages and no formulas." His idea became TOMS shoes.

   It was tough to get 250 prototype shoes made. But by the end of the first day the website was open for orders, they sold 2,220 pairs! They had promised a four-day delivery. That was great, except for the fact that they only had 160 pairs left. Blake and his partner Alejo quickly hired three interns off of Craigslist to call every person who ordered shoes and let them know they might have to wait up to eight weeks for delivery. Unbelievably, only one person cancelled their order.

   When Blake hit the streets of LA seeking retailers who would buy into TOMS and its concept, American

Rag was the first to say yes. He was fortunate to pitch TOMS to a shoe buyer who had seen more shoes than most people would see in a lifetime, therefore she had seen and heard it all. She realized that TOMS was more than a shoe – it was a story, and she loved the story as much as the shoes. From there it was one retail customer after another until they had given millions of shoes to children in need.

The great story of TOMS shoes carries the business and the cause. That is pretty brilliant. It has to feel incredibly fulfilling to have come up with the idea, figured out a solution, and have the results that TOMS has, countries apart no less.

Sadly, there are now knock-offs without a cause or copycats of the cause, but TOMS was first to market. Just as all passion workers and passionate companies, you have to ignore that and stay focused on your mission and purpose.

For Blake Mycoskie, TOMS was only one part of it. What he realized was his passion to start something that matters and how committed he felt to promote that idea so that more people would do the same. He decided to write the book *Start Something That Matters* as an inspiring guide for that idea, which would hopefully plant the seed in other people or other businesses. Is Blake Mycoskie making a difference in the world with his one and only life? I certainly think so.

"If you organize your life around your passion, you can turn your passion into a story and then turn your story into something bigger – something that matters" said Blake. Stories resonate with people more than facts. The other brilliant thing about the TOMS story is that customers love to tell others the story. For all of history, word-of-mouth advertising has been the best and least expensive way to sell a product. Brilliant.

Another cool company built on passion is a company who doesn't try to make you understand their story. Bert and John Jacobs' attitude is you either get it (Life is Good) or you don't, and it's not their job to talk you into it. The brothers started with an optimistic attitude, a simple slogan and a stick figure they slapped on a t-shirt. People responded to it and it became a national craze with the company artwork on shirts, hats, water bottles, pants, pajamas, and shoes. To just start a business and make tons of money wasn't appealing to them. From the very beginning, they both wanted to do something more meaningful with their lives.

The idea for Life is Good came from a brainstorm one day about how negativity permeates the world. They began brainstorming ways to combat it with optimism. "Trends have an ebb and flow, but the idea of seeing the glass half full is timeless." What they started to notice is people who faced the most adversity in life embraced the message the most.

"We believe a responsibly-run business for profit is one of the most influential tools for positive social change. We are the ones with resource, money and the public's attention because we have consumer product and services. We have a platform, and if you're willing to use that for the right things, that's really powerful." – Bert and John Jacobs of Life is Good

Passion workers are critical to our world. I wouldn't even want to imagine a world where people were just like robots and didn't care about humanity. When you talk with passion workers you quickly realize they aren't the even-keeled people who calmly motor along in life. They are the intense, giving it all you've got, heart broken when it doesn't work or they lose their passion for a while, and always get back on the high again kind of people. Passion workers contribute so much of themselves and to the world. It's exhausting and exhilarating. It's fun and frustrating. Every one of us has passion workers in our lives and the lives of our children who have shaped and changed us, as well as inspired and challenged us. Certain parents are passion workers if they take the enormous responsibility for what it is.

Passion workers get their fuel from a fire in their belly. Primarily, it's an internal motivation that might feel good externally, but that's not why they do it. Passion in business and causes needs to be promoted for the goldmine it is for the world. What can you do to inspire yourself further? What can you do to appreciate and inspire other passion workers? Is your passion unwavering or being tested? What can you do if you're questioning it? If your passion for work or a cause has come to an end, what's the best next thing you can do with your passion? Have you gotten an idea in this lesson to start something that matters? Most importantly, what are you going to do every day to stay committed as a passion worker in the world?

Lesson 8
Parenting Legacy!

Every parent will leave a parenting legacy no matter what they do. There is no way to avoid it and no parent is exempt. Your parenting legacy is simply how well you did the job of parenting. That might be exciting or scary to you depending on the quality of the legacy you are building. Yet every one of us will be judged, by our children at least and perhaps others, based on the impact our parenting had.

When we talk about "what will your children inherit from you?" we tend to think of financial assets, i.e. money, stocks, real estate, a business, or nothing. Falsely, we don't often realize they inherit something so much more critical that will last a lifetime from us as parents. Each parent writes on the slate of who the child is during their psychologically important formative years. How we nurtured (or didn't nurture) them doesn't disappear at 18. It can stay with them their entire life. Parents' impact will have a ripple effect throughout all the categories of their children's lives.

Just think of that from your perspective as a child. How did your parents do? What messages did you receive? What was good about their parenting? What harmed you by their parenting? Were your parents around? Could you count on them? Were they consistent? Were they harsh, passive or just right? Did you feel prepared for life when you left their home?

Change your thinking to your own children. Can your child come to you, no matter what, and talk with you about the trouble they are in or a tough decision they need to make? Is your child free to live their own life, or do you live vicariously through them with all the demands that come with that? Are you a good adult role model for your child and their friends? Do you understand that when you became a parent, your child became the priority, above yourself when necessary? Do you know you can't quit the parenting job, no matter how hard it gets? Do you know children become what they live and learned that from you?

All of this doesn't mean your children get to blame you for life based on how they were raised. At some point, they become independent adults who make their own choices and receive the consequences. If you're over 21, it's not mom and dad's fault anymore.

At a certain age your adult children have to be self-reliant. Yet for a strong parenting legacy you will remain in the "parent" role. The ING (parent**ing**) will fall off to become more of an adult friend to your child who serves a support role rather than actively directly their life. And at this stage, the parent/adult-child relationship should be an equal give and take, unlike the young child who only takes. In later life, if you have left a good parenting legacy, hopefully your child will return the love by caring for you in your elder days, if necessary.

Have you thought about your parenting legacy prior to reading this? Those who have a passion for parenting certainly have. They understand how critically important each day of parenting is from a profound-impact-on-life mindset. Parenting doesn't have to be intense at all times. There is also great joy in the parenting experience that is priceless for a lifetime. Children appreciate the silly times, lazy times, and ordinary days too. If your parenting is going the way you want it to, that's great – keep going.

If the concept of a parenting legacy has you thinking about some things you want to change, that's great too. The only time it's too late to change your parenting legacy is when you are no longer here. There are plenty of deathbed conversations between dying parents and their grown children. It doesn't have to wait that long. Every day is an opportunity to build your parenting legacy and our children (should they become parents) will have a chance to keep the things they liked about our parenting legacy and add their own with their children.

The one topic I swore I'd never write or speak about is my personal experience parenting. One of my writing friends tried for years to get me to write about it and I always immediately rejected the idea, although I openly wrote about pretty much everything else.

Finally he said, "What's the big deal? Why won't you write about parenting?" The answer falls in the same category as my fear of happiness – if I talk about parenting (my happiness), watch: my children will go wild and I'll wish I never shared anything. Besides, my children are teenagers, and teenagers want privacy. My friend kept prying.

"Now wait a minute. That's never going to happen. Whatever you are doing is successful – why wouldn't you be willing to share that with other parents?" After years of his pushing, and consent from my family, I decided to take the risk.

In no way am I a parenting expert, although I realize the way my husband and I go about parenting is unique. I come from a single-parent family, public housing, trailer parks and apartments. Andre comes from two stable married parents who always owned a home. We both were teachers before we were parents. In particular, I was a business and career teacher. These dynamics allowed us to pull from the best of these perspectives to be the kind of parents we are.

In hindsight, we are very fortunate to have the wide variety of experiences that have added to our approach. The strategies we use come from the first two sentences in the previous paragraph. This means I am merely sharing with you our mindset and the strategies that have been successful for us, so far in our journey of raising three children.

I am not telling you what to do as a parent, I am simply sharing what we do that it may give you something worthwhile to think about in your own life.

I like to think of my parenting commitment like my marriage vows – to have and to hold from this day

Lesson 8 – Parenting Legacy!

forward, for better or for worse, for richer, for poorer, in sickness and in health, to love and to cherish; from this day forward until death do us part. Most dedicated parents will experience all of this roller coaster of life with their child. Parenting is a big job, just like marriage, and you can't be in it when it's easy and quit when it's inconvenient. Something bigger than yourself connected you and your child. That parent connection was meant to be for a lifetime, as long as it's healthy.

This commitment reminded me that I had written a letter to each of my children in their baby book before they were born. Sometimes it's fun to look back as an experienced parent to what you were thinking when the journey began. "I want you to feel loved and safe...I promise to be supportive and encourage you to do your best...I want to be a good role model for you...When you are involved in activities, I promise to be your best cheerleader...When I make mistakes I hope you can forgive me... I will try my best to be a mom you can be proud of...You have given me so much by being a part of my life." I had no clue what I was getting into when I wrote that first letter, but I was professing my love, commitment, compassion, and excitement to the infant gifts God was giving me. Yet today I would say the same thing, in perhaps a more experienced way.

I wanted to be a mother since I was two. When I was a little girl I thought the greatest pleasure of motherhood was to have your own special someone to love forever. The week before I turned 29 and actually became a mother, I instantly realized it had nothing to do with me, and everything to do with the miracle baby God just trusted me with. Sixteen years into the journey, I know my main purpose on this earth is to be a mother for Mia, Dante and Lexi. If this is all I ever do in my lifetime, that will be enough.

It doesn't matter if anyone else or even my children understand. I know and understand the importance of me, a little girl from the ghetto, raising them to be wonderful human beings who are self-reliant, happy and making a difference in the world. It changes my family legacy.

I had no idea how much joy my children would be to me, nor how fulfilled I would feel having this experience with my own family. My dream was a mom, a dad, and children all intact for a lifetime, as I come from a multiple divorce family. My children don't need to be or do anything to get my unconditional love and acceptance. I love them simply because I have been blessed to be their mother.

One of the things I respect the most about Andre and I as parents is that we both give 110% effort to our commitment as parents. He changed as many diapers as I did. I do the morning shift and he does the evening shift, which used to be about babies and is now about supervision. Both of us want to have a 50-50 say in parenting decisions, and don't back down easily if we don't agree. We are hard on each other in terms of our expectations of each other as parents. We have our differences, but our values are the same. He's a good dad, and he would say I'm a good mom.

Our children have no doubt as to how much we love them. We are consistent, which lets our children know our expectations every time. As parents we each get one day off a year – Mother's Day or Father's Day – when we get to purely enjoy ourselves with our children. The parenting job we signed up for is a day-in and day-out commitment, 364 days a year, and we accept that. Giving 110% is probably the biggest factor in the way our children are turning out.

The other commitment that does affect our children is loyalty in our marriage. We both agreed and made a commitment to be loyal to each other. We both felt strongly enough about it that we would get divorced over it. When your primary value is – family first – you realize you are not just cheating on your spouse, you are having an affair on your entire family. It hurts the children as much, if not more, than the spouse. So a commitment to be loyal in my marriage is also a commitment to put my family first, above all else, every day. That builds a strong family.

A parent has two main purposes – **to nurture** (love, support, physically and emotionally care for) and **to prepare** the child to function in the world (to become self-reliant.)

Everyone can understand the first purpose. It's the second one that is critical for all children, but that many parents may not fully be aware of. Parents may grasp that their child has to eventually move out, yet they might not think about it from a functional standpoint in the midst of them mothering or fathering the child they love. A mother or a father naturally wants to take care of their dependent child. The ones who over-cater to every need and want are the ones who may not realize that can hinder their child's development and ability to function in the world on their own.

My gift was being a career teacher before I was a parent. It used to surprise me every spring at parent-teacher conferences how many parents would ask me, a teacher in my 20s, for my advice on how they should handle their 16-, 17-, or 18-year-old at home. I wasn't a parent, and it's completely different at school. However,

I realized work concepts like teamwork, pay for performance, work ethic, hard and soft skills work. Based on some of the chaos I was seeing in my students' families, whether that was from entitlement, passive parenting, dysfunction, or lack of caring, I realized one thing. Our greatest job as parents is to lovingly prepare our children to be self-reliant in the world. If I am a helicopter parent, they won't be prepared because I did everything for them. If I don't teach them, they won't be prepared because they won't know anything. If I'm a failing example, they will be prepared to fail.

So it was with this idea that "it's my job to prepare them for the world" that I approached parenting when it was my turn. I would ask myself, *What do they need to be able to do or know in order to* get into daycare, for example. Then I'd ask the question again before the next milestone: pre-school, kindergarten, middle school. Answering the question would easily produce a list that I could teach them and make sure they were prepared. Because my children were prepared mentally and socially, we didn't have difficulty transitioning at each stage. That saved a lot of stress for everyone.

As Mia started her freshmen year of high school I was ask to speak about my book *Pretendia: Smash the Glass Slipper and Awaken Your Best Self* at a Parent Connection meeting. I came up with this metaphor to teach them. If your job was to pack your child's suitcase for life, what are the essential skills, attitudes and knowledge you would make sure you packed for them? The parents then worked solo or with a parenting partner to create a list. The list became the guide for the next four years to make sure they accomplished the essential skills. The number-one question I got asked was, "What would be the first thing you would pack for your children?" My answer was resourcefulness. If I could only give them one thing, that skill could get them everything else they need.

I use to teach a tourism unit to my high school marketing students and then took them to Disney World for a weeklong internship. The students going had to raise the money, make all arrangements, get us there and back, and plan our itinerary. I purposely stood back and was available if they needed something, but I let them do everything.

Other teachers thought I was crazy and would never consider using that unconventional way of "teaching." What I knew was those students learned how to: raise money for something they really wanted, work together and work out conflict, how to work with adults they did not know and work out arrangements, how to travel by bus, plane and rental van, and most importantly, they saw adults who said yes to creativity and business.

I approach parenting the same way. My children will tell you, "She's always teaching us something," (that's the curse of being a former teacher's child). When they were little I would say every time, "say please," or "say thank you." My mother-in-law would tell me they don't have to say that every time (she meant to grandma), but I insisted. Now that they are teenagers and out on their own, teachers or other parents will tell me "your kids are always so polite." That's why I kept insisting. There are so many things and lessons I need them to know before they venture out into their own lives. They have heard the core reason I do this many times, "God trusted me to be your mom and I owe it to Him to do a really good job." In my defense, I'd like to say it's always good stuff I'm teaching them – time will tell.

At the foundation of our family is the idea that our sacred people live in our home. These are the people that matter the most to each of us, and they should be treated that way. Many people do the opposite – save their best behavior for when they are in public with mere strangers, then act the worst in privacy with their loved ones. This idea came to my attention a long time ago when a speaker said, "Only say to a loved one what you want printed in the newspaper (or on the Internet these days) with your name attached." Is it hard to do? Yes. Is it worth it, though? Yes. A home should be a safe place to fall and recoup from the busy-ness of life. Peaceful is nice. A warm and inviting space is so good for everyone. It makes it easier to go back into the world and be your best.

So on this line of thinking, we also don't accept siblings physically attacking each other. Does that make sense? I'm your brother or sister who loves you and I'm allowed to take my anger and frustration out on you physically just because we're family. If they did that to anyone else it would be completely unacceptable. It's unacceptable for family too.

You want the best for your sacred people. If you don't like the word sacred, replace it with "utmost importance." These are the people who are of the utmost importance in your life. You love and encourage them. They are your teammates in life. The better the team does, the better each member of the team is. Each member of the team must contribute. At every age children can contribute to the family.

Values are very personal. Our first value is family first as you have already read about. We also value education and show that in mom and dad continually educating themselves, as well as participating and monitoring each child's education. This includes getting a good night's sleep, eating brain healthy foods, regular workouts, a regular routine for homework, required weekly reading, monitoring their grades through an online software provided by our school district and encouraging and allowing any extra educational camp or activity they are interested in such as College for Kids. Our expectation is that they do their personal best rather than a certain grade. If they can look us in the eyes and say they did their very best, we'll accept that.

We believe each of us is here to make a difference in the world. Andre does that through coaching youth athletics and managing a large staff at work. I do that through speaking, writing, and personal interaction with people. It will be fun to see how each of our children chooses to make a difference as adults. But even in our community and neighborhood, we try to make a difference. That might be helping out a family in need, mowing a neighbor's yard, delivering bread to shelters, or helping a teacher. None of us are here to just take up space. One person, one gesture can make a difference. I've seen it happen many times.

Compassion for people is a family value. We live in a time and place where humankind is evolving and realizing that we are all connected in the world. I want my children to be happy, so how could I want anything other than your children to be happy? If I see someone hurting, how can I turn my head and walk away? If I know one small gesture on my part could make life easier for you, why wouldn't I do it? My belief is that people are here to help people, otherwise we'd live more isolated. In the end we all want the same thing for our families – to be healthy, happy and living a good life.

As no surprise to you, we value sports as a way to teach our children many life lessons. Teamwork, sportsmanship, dedication, doing your personal best, competition, strategy, the attitude of "never quit," victory, failure, perseverance, and the list goes on. Sports are one tool we use to help build our children's character. Andre's first chance to coach our children was t-ball and from there it was a blur of basketball, baseball, football, softball. The only sports Andre hasn't coached our children in are volleyball and lacrosse. Many kids perhaps wouldn't be happy with their dad coaching them, but to Andre's blessing, all three of them have been accepting of it.

Our oldest is the most like Andre, which you know can sometimes cause problems. It was actually coaching and working together that helped them turn the corner of their personalities being so similar. Now that Mia is older they enjoy laughing together over the same sense of humor that I often don't understand.

We have many other values we want to instill in our children. In order to not invade their privacy further I'll stop here and let you come to your own conclusions as you finish reading the book and get glimpses of who we really are as parents.

My children don't complain much, but if I really press them, they will say what they like the least is my high expectations of them. The last thing I want to do is raise perfectionists, since that is wasted energy and no fun. Yet, I also know from my teaching days that children will rise to meet your expectations if you treat them well and respect them. I'd rather support and encourage my children to meet high expectations rather than lower them to mediocrity. What would be worse is for a parent to have low expectations and the child meets them. That will crush a child's self-esteem and potential. When you approach parenting that way, neither you nor your child will ever know their full potential. My high standards always come with love and support to meet them. Would you rather your mother think nothing of you, or believe you can do anything you set your mind to and work hard at?

Think of your teachers or bosses who had low expectations of you. Did you prosper with them? Did you feel an internal drive to want to do your best, or did you feel uninspired and lifeless under their leadership? Parenting is no different. I lead by inspiring and encouraging. Others lead by criticizing what they don't want. But in the end high expectations, not low, is what brings out the best in people.

While we have high standards for our children, we want each one to be authentically themselves. Personality-wise, our three children are different, and we want to support that. We don't want them feeling like they have to be something or do something for us to love them. Decades of the average person's life are wasted on trying to be someone he is not. Typically, adults are in their 40s and 50s before they stop caring what anyone else thinks of them and start embracing who they really are. It would be so much easier if we encouraged people throughout their whole life to say "This is who I am," and boldly be and enjoy that.

To be obligated into a career you don't want is too long of a life sentence for anyone. Just think of how many hours we spend working as adults. That is too many hours to give away to something someone else wants you to do. Besides, we statistically know people in careers they dread are often depressed and lifeless. People who have chosen a career that fits who they are, along with their skill set and interests, are happier people in general. If my children are interested in careers that I lack knowledge in to help guide them, I'll happily reach out to someone with that expertise and appreciate any help they can offer. If we as parents feel we can only go as far as the expertise we currently have, we are going to limit our children in many aspects of their life.

A person's true self also evolves over a lifetime. At 18 they are just beginning to discover their likes, dislikes, personality, etc. A person's brain is not even fully developed until they are 25 years of age, which is why I tell my children they need to wait at least until then to marry so they make a wise choice. At certain ages the importance of that era also tends to color our authentic selves such as career, marriage and children in the 30s and empty-nesters in our 50s. The primary importance at any age is to feel as if you have the freedom to really be and express yourself. The blessing is to have people around you who embrace that.

Part of encouraging them to be their true selves is not wanting to hold them back in life because we'll miss them. Given their diverse interests, any one of the three or all three children could end up living across the country or in another country. We don't want them to feel like we are an anchor for them. I'd be the first to admit it would be hard to let them go and not worry about them. But I wouldn't want to make them less than they could be by keeping them close to home if they felt they wanted or needed to go.

A major concept Andre and I agreed on before we got married was that our children own their own lives. It is not our place, nor would we want to tell them what to do with it. They should have the pleasure of choosing a

Lesson 8 – Parenting Legacy!

college, career(s), where and how to live with whom, and whom to marry. I was raised by a mother who never decided any of those things for me and I appreciated that. Life is a gift, but it's not a gift if you try to control it the whole time. Until 18 we will guide them, but even as teenagers we let them decide as much as they can. Our home is a safe place to learn about mistakes and consequences while we can help them decide how to overcome them, and it's also a place to celebrate creativity and freedom of choices.

Now that you know some of our mindset about parenting, I'll share with you how we manage our family. Effectiveness has just as much to do with management style as it does attitude. We come from the idea that we have a dream for our family and our job as parents is to lead our family there. The antiquated parenting style of ruling your children by fear and forcing them to "respect" you is harmful and ineffective. If you lead your family with inspiration and are willing to do everything you ask them to do, a natural respect will develop. When we started out managing our family it was by trial and error, just like every other young family.

When our children were little we had to keep a close eye on them and constantly be teaching and showing them how we wanted them to behave. We would watch the movie *Lilo and Stitch* where the main message was "Ohana" which means, family = no one left behind. I used this to teach them to stay within my sight when we were out in the world. It started when Lexi was a newborn and Dante was two and half. I would put them in a double stroller and needed Mia to keep one hand on the stroller so I always knew where she was. If Mia let go Dante would say "Ohana" and that let Mia know we can't leave you behind, hang on. As they got older we dropped that word, but the deep meaning that we are a family and never going to leave anyone behind stayed as a family value. Even in middle school and high school they know we expect them to always look out for each other. This set the tone for us operating as a family unit.

From the time they were babies until kindergarten, so much of our life was about routines, telling, teaching, monitoring, exploring and physically loving them (hugs, kisses, saying I love you, and taking good care of them.) This stage was fun and physically exhausting. Now we know that stages only last for a few years, and by the time they are entering and advancing through elementary school they will become more and more physically independent, which makes it a lot easier.

Kindergarten through 5th grade was developing a foundation of good study habits, making good friends, learning sportsmanship, discovering their interests, and monitoring how they were doing. We were always aware of what they were doing, who they were with and how everything was going.

When our son, Dante (the middle child), went to middle school, I realized it was time for our first transition from baby parents to parenting older children who need more space and independence. We backed up a few steps and gave them more freedom and time with friends. We started teaching them about choices and consequences. There was enough room for them to make mistakes so we could teach them before they made bigger mistakes out in the world. The funny part is they make very few mistakes. – we need more teaching opportunities.

Freshman year of high school is a year to keep monitoring similar to middle school because there are so many choices, tons of new friends and older influences that can upset everything you've been working for so far. I'll never forget when Mia went off to high school and was playing three sports. Her days were often twelve or more hours away from home, and it was the first time since she went to kindergarten that I had growing pains (bittersweet heart pains.) I just missed her, but I was thrilled she was thriving. By the end of the year I got used to it, and knew every year would be a little more pulling away because that is what she is supposed to do.

When Mia became a sophomore in high school we knew we needed to transition again and give her more room and independence. The great part is she is so goal-oriented and self-directed she chooses to stay on a very focused path about what she's working for, and is not easily distracted by typical teenage trouble. We'll have to do the same for Dante and Lexi and they may handle the freedom differently. Each child earns how much freedom they have based on how well they handle it. That just makes sense, right?

Each year our children get more responsibilities and more freedom. To this point we have been blessed with almost zero issues with them as teenagers, which we know is remarkable. It is a testament to them and how well they have responded.

Each of them knows they can talk to me about anything and I'll be there to help them work it out. If they are having a problem and need to talk, they each have a different style of doing that. One of them wakes me up during the night when he/she can't sleep, another one of them talks best in the car, and another talks before bed. But the point is they are still talking to us. As long as your teenager is still talking to you about what is going on with them, you are doing all right.

We don't claim "mom and dad are the bosses so you do what we say" without regard for the children. Don't get me wrong, Andre and I are the final deciders and Mia, Dante and Lexi know we are the leaders of our family. How we operate as a family unit is when making individual decisions, like could Dante play hockey when he was in first grade, we considered how it would affect everyone in the family before we decided. In that case the answer was no. With three children we couldn't put that much time, money, and effort into one child. I also was not willing to favor our son over our daughters.

Believe me, Dante was not happy when it seemed to him every boy in his class was playing hockey. He even spouted back at me "Well, when I'm 18 I'm going to play hockey!" and then he added, "And you can't come watch me!" He was upset and felt I was being unfair to him. At 14 he doesn't even remember hockey or talking to me like that. It was the right decision for our family at the time.

Often times when one of my children wants something I respond with the fact that I have three children not just one to consider. Yet, I do take into consideration that my children are very different and what would be the best given the situation if I could do what they needed or wanted. Andre has always laughed at how fair I always try to make everything. To this day, if we are at the mall and Dante and Lexi want a gumball, I give Mia a quarter because she never wants a gum ball. I don't want her to miss out. I know that's silly, but it matters to me.

Lesson 8 – Parenting Legacy!

Now that they are older it's harder to keep things exactly the same in regard to being "fair." In certain categories we have to treat them differently in order to treat them the same. Each of our children may care about something totally different. Dante, for example, wanted to play AAU basketball on a traveling team an hour and half away from our home. This meant a large commitment of time, travel and money for a certain period of time. Mia had an opportunity to go to Disney's ESPN center in Orlando with the varsity softball team, and this was at the same time the other two children had state basketball tournaments. We agreed to let Mia go and had to tell the other two we can't go along this time. Lexi has to understand that she's younger and she'll get her turn for these things if she wants them, but right now she'll settle for competitive county basketball and the mall.

Our children know their heritage, customs and traditions. Andre's the one who is big about that. Even when I wasn't interested in where I come from, Andre pushed me to learn more about it. He wanted me to talk to my grandma before she passed and my aunt on my biological dad's side so we could preserve the Native America records of my dad's descendants and the tracts of land we own on a reservation in North Dakota. With my sister's help, we have our children registered in the tribal records so they can receive money for college. Andre's always been interested in genealogy, and I wouldn't have done any of that without his gentle urging.

The Michaels side is large and centered in the Midwest. We regularly see grandparents, aunts, uncles and cousins. My mom has always lived in the same town as us, and she is that third parent whenever we need one. Andre's grandmothers are both still living at 99 and 96 and the children see them whenever we go to Andre's hometown.

Speaking of traditions, I've always learned from the parents ahead of me. I pay attention to the good, the bad and the ugly and then choose what's right for my family. For example, when I was teaching at Middleton High School, I learned from John Sibley, a business education teacher, the "I buy the needs, you add to the wants" concept. He explained with his children he bought the needs so when they need a pair of tennis shoes he would give them what a decent pair of tennis shoes would cost him, say $50. If his son wanted the latest Nike "must have" customized shoes, KDIV, and they cost $150, his son would need to pay $100 if he wanted them.

That makes good sense to me, because the one thing I know from teaching high school and college is kids generally don't care when it's their parents money. They care when it's their own money. Who were the kids that didn't get their security deposit or textbook rental back? The ones whose parents paid for it. So we adopted John's idea and it works well for us.

We have been able to get our children to care about family money to a large degree by explaining money to them. We don't have a problem getting our change back when we have given one of our children a twenty to go out with friends or money for a tournament. They know if they don't give the change back they won't get any money next time.

We all are responsible for maintaining the home we live in so it grows in value and if we don't we won't live here, so the kids have to help with the yard and upkeep. We have offered to downsize many times and they prefer to stay here and help. We spend our money based on who needs something not on who wants something. The most common item right now is "Who needs a pair of tennis shoes?"

If you're thinking rich parents can provide a better parenting legacy than a parent on the low end of the socio-economic scale – that's not necessarily true. If you fill your child full of stuff, create an entitlement attitude and are never around because you're "working," your child may not receive a positive legacy. There are plenty of parents at the low income level who provide love, support, encouragement, and life lessons that will serve their children well and leave a positive parenting legacy. Just as there are parents at the middle-class and wealthy who do the same thing. The point is that a high-quality parenting legacy is not defined by money.

Right now I'm paying attention to how people are paying for college, as the need will be coming up soon. Almost right away we will have two in college at the same for years. Andre's parents helped him and his siblings pay for college. My mom couldn't afford to and my adoptive dad refused to pay. Andre and I are planning on a hybrid approach. As a family we have three children to get through college, and that's how the decision will be made.

Instead of my usual "everything has to be even approach" we have to go with the idea that it's an investment partnership with each child. So when Mia goes it will be a partnership effort between her dad, myself and her. It's up to the three of us to get her through. We are very flexible and open as to how each semester or year will go depending on how she is doing and costs. Then it will be an investment partnership with Dante, his dad and I. Finally it will be an investment partnership with Lexi, her dad and I. Can you see the difference when you have to answer to an investment partner at the end of each semester as to their willingness to continue investing in you rather then not showing your grades to mom and dad and expecting them to keep paying?

We are open to anything between paying the first two years so they have a good foundation and are on their way to not quitting college, to paying based on grades, to paying cash, to letting them take a loan and helping them pay it, to scholarships, to sponsorships, to paying the last two years so they'll finish, etc. No matter what, we are not choosing to pay the full bill because we believe they have to have skin in the game to win.

Andre took five years to graduate and I took four because I took 16-18 (because I only had to pay for 12) credits a semester and 12 credits in the summer (because I only had to pay for 6.) I worked the whole way through college, and Andre played college basketball and baseball. Andre also worked in the summer and during his 5th year of college.

The arrangement may be different for each child based on their need and ability. That's where we will be treating them differently in order to treat them the same. For example, if one or some are able to get scholarships, more of our money will go to another child. If you have any tips on paying for college, feel free to e-mail them to me. I would appreciate it.

We are also going to tell them the truth about college. The purpose of college is to let you grow up as an adult (Can you imagine 18-year-olds working full time in the business world?) and prove to yourself that you can do things you never thought you could get through. It is to get specialized training so that you can get a job or become an entrepreneur when you are finished. It is up to you to make it a valuable experience that will help you do that, and not just be an expensive field trip we wish we hadn't taken. I'll also tell them the secret to my college success – study your butt off Sunday to Thursday so you can have fun on the weekend, and set a GPA goal for each semester.

Our children know parents are human and make mistakes just like everyone else. Mia has heard me say so many times, "We mess up the most with you because you were first." She knows we don't mean to, like when I used to struggle for an hour and half to get her to nap because I thought all kids had to nap until they were five. Our pediatrician, Dr. Bernhardt, finally asked me "How long does she nap when you finally get her to sleep?" and I tearfully whimpered, "Less than an hour." He looked at me and said, "Well, seems she's done napping and you are wasting your time." Lexi, the youngest, was done napping by three. Sorry Mia!

Or the fact that we had Mia take her driver's education class online because we thought it would be easier with her busy softball schedule. Nope! Turns out it's a ton more work than taking the class at 4 Lakes. Dante and Lexi will take the class.

And finally, Mia got her driver's license two months after her sixteenth birthday because we didn't realize she had to have her temporary license for six months before she can take her driving test. She was really good about it, but I felt terrible. We certainly have messed up with Dante and Lexi too, but the point is our children have forgiven us because they know the errors weren't intentional.

One of the rules we have always had is no parent

splitting. Our children are not allowed to ask one parent and if they don't get the answer they want, go ask the other parent. Since they were three years old they have understood this rule. Andre and I have to present a unified partnership, or they would work on splitting us up as parents. You see it all the time. Who's the parent children ask for money? Who's the parent children ask for privileges or to bend the rules? Guess who loses with parent splitting? Everyone. The parents end up fighting, and the children end up running the family and having no leadership. There have been times when Andre and I don't agree and yet, because of this commitment, we both have to present a unified front.

Mia, Dante and Lexi may not like that rule, but they know they get a policy that makes the rule easier and that is we have open communication. There is no topic or conversation that is off limits. Since they were little, we have let them ask any question they want to. One of the funniest videos of Lexi is when she was three years old and we had a dog named Buster. Out of the blue Lexi asked, "Does Buster celebrate Jewish?" Andre, having respect for her question, calmly answered "No. Buster is Catholic like us." They know we will talk calmly about anything on their mind, so their questions are no big deal. They will ask at home in the kitchen, on errands at a store, and most often when we are driving somewhere. (I think that's because we aren't looking at them when we're talking.) Religion, money, criminals, addictions, taxes, medical topics, discrimination, etc. are completely welcome conversations in our home.

Many parents won't talk about what makes them uncomfortable. Here's what changed our minds about that: if teenagers want to do something or know

Lesson 8 – Parenting Legacy!

something, they will go where they can get answers. Who do they most often go to? Their peers. Do you really want your most uncomfortable topics answered by immature teenagers (No disrespect – they just haven't lived enough life yet)? Are you really going to hand your child over to that group, turn your head and hope all goes well? That is how completely non-factual urban legends get started. Or are you going to be a grown up and realize the consequences are too high if you don't face your discomfort and handle it? Your children may feel uncomfortable too, but they will eventually respect you for your open communication.

Do you know one of the top complaints of children? Parents who don't practice what they preach. Here's another piece of wisdom from my teaching days. Students and children lose respect when they see the adult in charge telling them one thing and doing another. "Be honest and don't steal." Yet then they see mom receiving too much change at the store and putting it in her purse without saying anything, or they hear mom and dad talking about hiding income from their taxes. For the child that creates a "why should I if you don't?" mentality. They don't accept the "I'm a grown up, you're a child" answer to this dilemma.

"Actions speak louder than words" is the answer. Our children need to see us doing exactly what we are teaching them to do. Andre and I don't ask our children to do anything we won't do ourselves. Certainly there are things we can do as adults that our teenagers can't do, especially regarding the law. Yet they see us still handling our responsibilities. So we choose to stay up late and have a few drinks, but they see us get up in the morning and handle our usual responsibilities. We also don't do that often, so they see us socially drinking responsibly. More of what our children do see us doing is working, spending time with family, enjoying our passions, and living a good life.

At times, it's not easy being a parent. We all get tired and experience days where we are feeling like we can't have one more thing go wrong. But quitting is not an option for a parent. Every one of us needs an extended support system and an adult we trust to step in and give us a break now and then. We have purposely built-in family, friends, neighbors, Godparents, and legal guardians, should we need them, to help us as parents. All of these people try to practice what we preach to our children. In real life, adults make an occasional mistake, but for the most part we need to model for children the way we want them to behave.

People Support What They Help to Create – was a valuable lesson I learned at the age of 17 at a DECA Leadership Lab. This concept works professionally, personally, and socially. The concept is that people will support what they have an opportunity to create, such as mission, vision, rules, projects, etc. It is the opposite of dictating. If we as a family decide where we are going on vacation, how we're going to get the money, and what we are going to give up, if necessary, to get the vacation, our children will support it. If we instead told them "here's how your summer is going to go," we may get some disgruntled children who don't feel like cooperating. When children have a chance to give input on their lives, they rebel less. Dictating parents often have teenagers who rebel for this very reason. Again, this management style of parenting is democratic and for older children, but it has worked well for our family. Andre and I lead the process but Mia, Dante and Lexi get to participate as much as possible given the situation and their ages.

Where we have dictated as parents is in setting boundaries for our children. They have always had set bedtimes, requirements about friends and having friends over, limits on what and how much they can spend, the expectation that school comes first, and limits on technology. No violent video games. Leave your cell phone in the kitchen overnight (this avoids texts at all hours of the night. Teenagers need sleep).

Yep, I was the parent that asked the first time my child played at your home, "Do you have a gun in your home?" until I was sure my children were old enough to not touch it. I knew first-hand why I had to ask this question – my dad's cousin accidently shot his best friend in front of my dad when they were 12.

We won't be serving underage drinkers, and our teenagers won't be having/attending any co-ed sleepovers. We are the parents, not our children's want-to-be-cool friend. Our job is to draw a line on what's appropriate at their ages. Plus, I'm not going to jail for anybody.

Even if children hate boundaries, boundaries keep kids safe. We understand this when they are little. "Don't cross the street without mom or dad," "Only use the stove with adult supervision," and "Tell mom or dad if you see danger." Yet somehow when our children become old enough to stay home alone, we think they don't need boundaries or supervision anymore.

Middle schoolers need as much supervision as ten-year-olds, and high schoolers may need as much supervision as five-year-olds because they encounter some pretty enticing opportunities. That doesn't mean I need to cramp my child's style and sit next to them everywhere they go. It means I know exactly who they are with, what they are doing, and proof that I can trust them. We trust our teenagers until they show us we can't. The more responsible they are, the more freedom they get.

I have chosen to be a parent who works out of our home because when I'm around, we don't get many surprises. I'm available for spur-of-the-moment conversations or needs. For the most part, my children are very independent and I think that's because they know the boundaries and also get a lot of freedom.

Every once in a while, people will ask us if we spanked our children. The answer is no. As I said earlier, we don't want to teach our children if someone loves you they have a right to hit you. That is especially confusing to little children. Both Andre and I were spanked as children, and each of us feels differently about it. Since that era, it has been proven that spanking is ineffective. Spanking is truly the adult out of control and at their wits end. If it teaches anything, it teaches the child to fear, not respect, their parent. The other question we get is "Do you ground your teenager?" No, we have never had to. That is another practice that seems to be ineffective and a bigger hassle for the parents.

What we do instead is parent with their currency. A child's currency is what they really care about, and losing the currency would matter enough to change the child's behavior so they can get the currency back. The currency may be the same or different for each of your children and the currency may be different at ten years of age and 17. We haven't had much of this either (because they learn quickly), but so far it has been loss of video games, iPod or phone. Lose of driving privileges may be effective for a teen with a license.

So that's pretty much the whole picture on how we manage our family. Obviously, I can only share with you up to the parenting point I am at. However, I have confidence because of the rapport we have built with our children so far and the effectiveness our style has produced that it will continue. I have faith in our children.

Finally, we need to teach them life skills, as I've been telling you. Life skills come in two varieties, hard skills and soft skills. Soft skills are personal traits, social graces, emotional intelligence, attitude, characteristics, etc. Soft skills complement hard skills, which are the technical skills required to do a job. A simple example would be a doctor. Medical training would be an example of hard skills, and bedside manner would be an example of soft skills. For the most part, our children will learn hard skills through formal and informal education and on the job because they probably won't choose the same professions Andre and I did.

Characteristics we are instilling in our children are being grateful, resourceful, creative, and resilient, and having an impressive work ethic and a sense of adventure. Those will serve my children well in life. And I absolutely want to add Andre's values of loyalty, The Golden Rule, sportsmanship, a home, and consistency. If I play my cards right, 18 years of solid development should give them the foundation of all of these essential characteristics.

They will need social and emotional intelligence. Social intelligence will give them the skills to be able to get along with others and know how to behave in each social setting they find themselves in. It will also allow them to have good friends, as well as be one. And hopefully it will give them good relationship skills so their personal and professional lives can be rich. Emotional intelligence is critical to help them deal with all of the emotional things, both good and bad, that they will go through in a lifetime. For example, they need to know how important positive self-talk is and how to deal with a crisis.

Our children need to know they always have personal power, no matter what is happening in their lives. They can go after what they want in life and get it. They can change their lives if they want to. Even if a situation looks hopeless, they still have the power to choose their attitude. Personal power supports confidence, and confidence can allow a person to go through life knowing they can handle anything that comes their way.

We are also teaching them to set and achieve goals. The ability to do that is critical in life, and yet most parents never teach this success tool to their children even if they use it themselves.

Most importantly, I tell my children I love them and give them a hug twice a day, before school and before bed. It may seem insignificant, but it is actually very important. If you are sent off to school knowing your parent loves you, unconditionally, it makes you feel secure. And if you know your parent loves you, unconditionally, before you go to sleep, it relaxes you and feels secure. Shockingly, one of the greatest human fears is "Am I lovable?" I am certain that my children know they are lovable, without question.

Well, I have shown you my passion for parenting, the lesson I was most intimidated to write. My children have not gone wild and made me regret it. This just goes to show you that what our children really care the most about is that we are willing to try our best. If they'd dare admit it, they want our love, stability and guidance before they leave home. They can understand that parents make mistakes and they can learn to forgive us. If we're lucky, they will want to continue the relationship when they are adults. They don't have to, and that's why if we want to be a parent for a lifetime we have to learn to transition the relationship as they get older.

Daily, my children hear "I love you very much and always." The "very much" is to remind them how intensely I love them and the "always" is to remind them **no matter what** they can always come to me and I'll be there for them. For me, it has been my greatest blessing to be allowed to serve as a mother for Mia, Dante, and Lexi.

All of these stories, concepts, and ideas are my parenting legacy. They will leave behind my thoughts and impression of what I believed to be a good parent, or at least a parent who tried and loved her children immensely. Every effort, decision, and joy has come from my passion for parenting.

My "WHY" comes from knowing that each child who is delivered to this world can make a difference. Each child deserves a solid start in life, and my heartache is for each child who starts in such unfair circumstances that I worry how they'll ever have a chance in life. By now I know I can't save every child or take them all home with me. But I can do my very best with the three children I was trusted with and maybe inadvertently inspire others to care enough to make a difference in a child's life, whether the child is theirs or not.

We all leave a parenting legacy, whether you are aware of it or not. I want to inspire you, if I haven't already, to be the best parent you can possibly be because it makes a profound impact on your children for their lifetime and your grandchildren after that. As long as you are alive, it is never too late to improve as a parent. Are you happy with your parenting legacy today? How can you make it even better because it matters that much? Please join me as a passionate parent.

Lesson 9
Having Fun!

Isn't that a great picture? The minute I saw it, I knew I wanted it for this book. It's so fantastic, first because of the look on Jeff's face. You can tell he just jumped on that child's bike, let loose, and had fun. And the second thing that grabs your attention about that photo is what a surprise it is to see a guy of Jeff's stature, 6'5", on an old fashioned child's bike with a banana seat. His buddy Dave had the presence of mind to grab his camera and captured the moment, which has brought laughs for a lot of people who get to enjoy it. When is the last time you jumped on a child's bike and let yourself have a thrill like back then? Jeff's photo is a great reminder to not be so grown-up that you miss the fun in the moment.

There are two things you have to be able to do when it comes to having fun – let go of control and don't be so serious. Have you ever thought about that before? Children aren't used to controlling things. That's why they can so easily have fun. When we are controlling things, we aren't usually having a ton of fun. Often, we are holding our breath and trying to manipulate others and ourselves to get the goal we have decided is of supreme importance at the expense of anyone else's wishes. Does that sound like fun? Trying to control fun is like wearing a turtle neck sweater to the beach: sweaty, awkward, and restricting.

We don't really have as much control over things as we like to pretend we do, anyway. There are variable factors we can't control all the time. We can either let our time, energy, and focus be consumed by the need to control, or we can learn to let it go for a more enjoyable life.

Parties are supposed to be fun, right? You can tell a lot about a host by the way they react and behave at their party. The control freaks are the ones having a fit in the kitchen because so-and-so ate the whatever off the buffet table before it was "appropriate to do so." They spend the whole party upset with the people they invited to the party because they aren't doing exactly what she wants them to do.

The fun hosts enjoy throwing a party for the joy it brings their guests. They do all of the prep work for the party, but when the party actually begins they happily allow their guests to do as they please. There are no meltdowns or broken friendships over etiquette. You can see the host smiling often while she enjoys her guests enjoying themselves.

Are you willing to give up a little control in order to have more fun in your life?

What I discovered while I was writing this book is that caution around happiness wasn't unique at all. In fact, it was very common in adults who come from a culture of deep scarcity – never feeling safe, certain or sure enough. Nope, it wasn't just the low-income people who came from this scarcity mentality. It was just as much the millionaires and the middle class who didn't feel safe, certain or sure enough to trust happiness. Scarcity and fear drive the caution of happiness.

Waiting for the other shoe to fall, playing the "what if" the worst happens game, constantly waiting for the bad news seems like odd behavior and it is –common, but odd. People who have a habit of planning for the worst are trying to prepare themselves in an attempt to lessen the pain, in case it ever happens. What they are thinking in theory doesn't actually work. When your spouse dies it is going to hurt just as bad as if you rehearsed the pain every day in your mind. The self-destructive game of believing you'll be prepared if it happens or relieved when it doesn't happen is not worth it. Expecting the worst won't even prepare you.

Author Brenè Brown calls this concept foreboding joy. Those two words get your attention, don't they? Preventing joy as to minimize vulnerability doesn't work. As a human being, there is no way to escape vulnerability. We can't get away from it, so we have a choice to make. Do we want to forebode joy or soften to a point where we surrender to joy?

When you feel or notice yourself doing this, say something simple like "accept joy" or "allow joy" to gently remind yourself to stop foreboding joy. The secondary reason we want to change this behavior is because adults pass it on to children. "Be a gracious winner, because next time you may be the loser," "Enjoy it now, because you're going to get hips like your mother," "It's great you got that scholarship, but college is a ton more expensive than that," or my grandma's comment warning me to be careful with happiness because when haters hear about it they'll hate you for it. My grandma was probably taught that by someone who was taught that by someone. I have discovered that it is about the person saying it and their own feelings – it's not even about you. So we need to catch ourselves passing on this fear of happiness, because it's an unfair thief. And if anyone cautions you about happiness, you need to keep right on doing what you are doing and ignore them.

For me personally, the idea of trusting happiness was an unfair expectation to start with. All you can trust about joy is that it will come and go in moments. That's life. I can choose to be happy most days, but some days it's not even appropriate to be happy, i.e. trauma, deep loss, etc. Ninety percent of the time, I'm happy and optimistic. Yet I know I'm capable of another 5% if I'd simply surrender to it and stop trying to hide it from others to protect myself from mean-spirited people. So after learning everything I have to this point, I will attempt it.

It does feel vulnerable to put yourself out there, but it can also be fun. By putting myself out there I have been invited to do all sorts of cool things, met great people and developed my talents. Do you have a fun list? Not a bucket list, but a list of things you think would be fun to try? Your list might be crazy things, sensible things, or anywhere in between. It doesn't matter if anyone likes your fun list. No one but you gets to approve your fun list.

Fun doesn't have to be the big things all of the time. What are the simple things that are fun for you? They can be incredibly simple, like chewing gumballs. One winter day when I didn't feel like going anywhere in the snow, I decided to stay home and paint the columns between the living room and kitchen the same deep lipstick red as the kitchen backsplash. I had lived in the house long enough that I had run out of colors to try. I put on one of Mia's Taylor Swift CDs and popped a couple gumballs in my mouth. Gumballs always make me think of middle school when I used to chew Hubba Bubba and the smell drove my mom nuts. I didn't mean to annoy her, I just loved the gum and blowing bubbles. I had a great time dancing, blowing bubbles and painting when no one was home. I do give Andre credit, as he never says anything when he comes home and I've painted.

It is hard to have fun when you're feeling stressed. We have a lot of stress in Western culture from the way our world has evolved into a materialistic, over-scheduled, capitalistic society – not to mention the economy. It has become common for Westerners to seek practices such as yoga and meditation, as well as study Eastern philosophy. For about the last year, I found myself contemplating the opposing views of Western and Eastern cultures to find a more peaceful way to approach life in the modern world we live in.

My first real studying of some of this philosophy came in the form of a multi-week webcast by Oprah Winfrey with author Eckhart Tolle regarding his book *A New Earth*. We needed Oprah to help us understand this unusual author who was living a Zen life in the

West. He was so calm he appeared almost comatose with his incredibly flat affect. No matter what they were talking about, he didn't change his monotone voice or outward energy. At one point Oprah said, "Do you even get excited?" Eckhart said, "Oh, yes. This is excited." He said it like you might say "This is a piece of bread" – no emotion compared to the way most people express emotions. His demeanor never changed over the ten weeks of the webcast, no matter what he was talking about.

Eckhart was describing that you can choose to stay calm and at peace no matter what is happening if you understand his philosophies. Eckhart and I would be extreme opposites when it comes to personal expression and energy.

What intrigued me was him saying that he has not been upset in years and he has lost his ego. Being upset and the ego rob so much joy in life that I wanted to understand him and how he was thinking. Was it possible to have a major disagreement with someone in an argument and just "leave it there" meaning you don't react, get involved or try to change the other person? That's tough stuff. It requires that you are very present and mindful at all times, which is no easy feat, at least for me.

There have been plenty of times where I have been able to do that and choose to not get my energy involved with things that don't matter in the grand scheme of things. Then there are other times where I have failed at that so miserably and exploded because I felt so strongly about an injustice or something I care deeply about. When that happens I often felt frustrated with myself that I had stepped in the trap and done exactly what Westerners do, the opposite of Eastern

Lesson 9 – Having Fun!

philosophy. A friend would say "Sofia, anyone would have been furious about that. You're being too hard on yourself." Struggling, I wasn't sure if that was right or if I was missing the Zen point.

Since 2008 I have read several books by experts on Eastern philosophy such as Wayne Dyer, Deepak Chopra, and His Holiness The Dalai Lama. What's a little funny to me is these Zen, unattached to anything authors, are making millions in our capitalist country by telling us how to be Zen. Is there a conflict of interest there, an oxymoron, or just a goldmine of desperate people?

So meditation is an ironic attempt for Westerners to try desperately to achieve which is exactly the problem. You don't achieve meditation, you practice it. Trying to get the hang of it with our ever-wandering minds can feel like trying to get pantyhose on an elephant. Yet those who can figure it out do feel a sense of peace and calm while they use the technique to relieve stress in their everyday life. So far I have been able to use and enjoy active meditation (meditation for ADHD people) which really does help a lot. The two forms I use most are a five-mile walk in the country by myself, with no music, dogs or any other distraction while I just focus on nature.

The other one I use is ten-pound dumbbell weights in the living room where I lay on my back and in slow motion do arm exercises while I focus on my breathing. I especially like to do that one if I'm writing a lot, or if something in particular is causing me to worry. They are both great techniques to help me get centered, release tension, and feel gratitude.

And, of course, there is yoga, which to date I have used more as stretching rather than a full routine and workout. My fondness for yoga developed when Lexi came home from school in first grade and said "Mom, we did yoga today in gym. Do you want to see the turtle pose?" She proceeded to fold her little body up into the cutest little bundle, and I was hooked. From that point she started teaching me what she was learning, and we would do it together on the living room or my bedroom floor. Every once in a while she would say, "Do you want to do yoga?" And I try to say yes as often as I can, because I know this special time with her will one day pass and I want to treasure it in the moment. It's great to have my own little yogi.

So, I have been learning and trying a few Eastern philosophies for the past four years, and like I said, I had come to a place of confliction in the last year. Does Eastern culture really work for the problems with Western culture, is Eastern culture the answer to Western culture or are they just two worlds apart? Friends have made comments like "Sure it works, if you get rid of all of the people in your life. Then I can be as Zen as Tolle and nothing can annoy me," or "I'm really good at being mindful until something really ticks me off," or "I have a house full of kids and stuff to deal with. Realistically, we couldn't live in one room with a bed and one blanket."

In the past month, I have come to this conclusion out of being too hard on myself for not mastering Eastern ways in my U.S. life. It is an unrealistic expectation when you live in the West – meaning it's not possible unless you are a monk or a nun living in a monastery. When I am a wife, mother of three and own two businesses, I can't plead Zen and be disengaged. I wouldn't even want to, because that would be to deny so much of what I am passionate about, and passion

Lesson 9 – Having Fun!

isn't Zen. So with that understanding, I do appreciate that there are techniques I can use that are helpful, relaxing and even fun; however, with my personality, with who I choose to live and where, that quest is not for me.

There are certainly parts of being present and mindful that have been invaluable. One of them is detaching to the outcome at Mia, Dante and Lexi's sporting events. I figured out pretty early on that if I didn't want to be stressed through the whole game for over 110 games a season, I better learn to be present and mindful. As a parent, my role is to support my children. I understand that I can't affect the game from my seat as an adult. Of course, I want my children's team to win so they will be happy. But the bigger gains of the game are what I am after, like sportsmanship, team effort, do your best, etc. I am raising good human beings first, not athletes.

So the first year I started this, I had to remind myself several times per game to relax and let it go. It wasn't that I didn't care I just needed to practice not being so engaged that I went on the roller coaster of up and down and twisting around with each turn of the game that made my stomach sick and produced a headache. The outcome of the game was the same if I did that or I sat peacefully and enjoyed my children with their teammates doing something they loved. The second option is so much better for me, and is how I survive in a sports family. Don't get me wrong, I want Mia, Dante and Lexi to have a fierce fire in their bellies which is the passion to go after what they want in life. I just don't need to live all their emotions with them.

Instinctually, last year, I let out a huge "THANK YOU!" when we really needed a basket and the ball went in the hoop. It was how I felt – grateful for the team. The crowd laughed at my odd use of those words on a basketball court. It was not like I was yelling "AMEN JESUS!" every time a basketball went in, but you would have thought so based on the looks and laughter I got.

This year I got over my shyness in saying that and saved my heartfelt "THANK YOU" for game-changing baskets. When I use it, I really mean thank you for that basket. Don't all athletes like to be appreciated? Grateful is just who I am, in the stands or not.

Sports are fun for my children to play and fun for Andre to coach. That is how he has bonded with each of them. Andre is very fortunate that all three of his children have a strong interest in sports. At their ages Mia, Dante and Lexi probably don't realize yet what a gift they have given their dad to allow him to be such a huge part of their lives. I appreciate their generosity.

More of the trouble we get into with fun is that not everyone enjoys the same kind of fun. Andre, Mia, Dante and Lexi all enjoy amusements parks and rides. I am a puker on roller coasters. So I have learned to take a book and enjoy the shade while they go have their fun. Then we'll do something we all enjoy together.

The ugliness of fun is when someone is selfish about it unless he has no one else in his life. To spend all of your time, resources, and energy in the pursuit of your fun to the point where there is nothing left for anyone else is sad. Of course, anyone who would do that is not a true partner. So I recommend that you have your fun, but also be aware of others in your life. Didn't we all learn to play nice when we were little? That rule still applies throughout life.

One day, my son said he didn't think adults have

Lesson 9 – Having Fun!

fun anymore. I must have shot him a panicked look, and he responded with "I know you and dad do, I mean normal people." Ha! I was happy that we were doing a good job – bring on the adult fun! There are plenty of times Andre and I bust out doing something crazy at home, and the kids are glad no one else saw it. We have hit the stage where a couple of them give some comments to the effect of "parents don't do that anymore." I think they mean age more than parent. But the thing is, if we give up certain things that are fun for us just to make them happy, we wouldn't be doing that for the right reason. Then, at 80 and 90, we think it's great when people are doing those silly things again. I, for one, will be keeping any of the fun I like to have, thank you. My fun card can't be revoked, and nor should anyone else's.

One of my reminders about the fact that important don't always equal serious is a framed photo I have in the living room. It's a picture when Mia was three years old, Dante was two and half years old and Lexi was four months old. They were all in their pajamas and I put the classic round plastic black glasses, bushy eyebrows and black mustache from Party City on each of them.

Dante's hands were on his knees with his toes curled up, and his mouth was wide open as he was laughing so hard his eyes were closed. Lexi was a little lump who couldn't sit up herself. She was starting to slump to her left toward Mia. Her eyes fit right in the middle on the eyeglasses but the nose looked huge on her face, and the mustache came to the bottom of her face. Mia was in a pink satin nightgown, her hair was shiny and perfectly in place, and her mustache covered her whole mouth, but her eyes were twinkling. These three little babies were so important to me, but this picture is obviously not serious.

If fun is in your day somewhere, every day, you are blessed. Fun can be for five minutes, a half hour, or hours. If we'd let go of serious a little bit, there would be more room for having fun. What's the harm in that? The main thing adults are afraid of when it comes to fun is embarrassing themselves. It all stems from children laughing at them, not with them, when they were children. Fear of embarrassment, or really humiliation, prevents fun. Well, I know a remedy for that – learn to laugh at yourself. We are going to look like idiots at times. Seeing an adult go flying on their behind while rollerblading as her cell phone launches into the air looks funny because it's unusual. People may laugh. Do you really want the worry of that happening to stop you from rollerblading?

People who are having fun in their lives are happy people. Fun and happy might seem frivolous at first glance. Yet they are essential for our health and longevity, and also for doing more good for our families, businesses, communities and ultimately the world. There is researched proof of this through the movement of positive psychology, which focuses on glorifying people's strengths rather than trying to fix people's weaknesses. The happier people are, the healthier they are. It makes sense – when we are happy our bodies secrete chemicals, including oxytocin, dopamine and serotonin, which regulate our immune system. That is why Eastern culture says we are our own pharmacy to heal our bodies, unlike Americans who want to pop a pill for instant relief no matter what.

Think about the statement – happy people are healthier, they live longer, and they do more good for their families, businesses, communities and ultimately the world. That right there is a whole lot of reasons to get happy and have fun in your life. Just look at that statement. Who in your community or circle of people have lived a long time? Were they happy during their lives? Did they have fun with their lives? Think about the people doing good for their families. How many can you think of who had fun doing it? Look at successful, impactful businesses and communities. Are they all work and no fun? Widen your thinking to people who have changed the world in big and small ways – I'll bet they aren't serious 100% of the time.

How satisfied are you with your life? When I asked myself that question in 1999, I said a six out of ten because I was capable of so much more. Today, I would say a healthy eight. A ten is reserved for the end of my life when I hopefully can say I gave the experience everything I had and am satisfied.

A study on happiness stated that people who are satisfied or better about their life are in a good mood 80% of the time. I thought that was low, as I feel like 90% or better. Do you fall in the good mood category? What would it take to get higher if you aren't already at 80%?

What might surprise you is that feeling challenged is an important component to satisfaction. I know that's true for me. I don't like pointless challenges like Andre getting a kick out of annoying me. But I need a few challenges that excite me now and then to feel fully alive. It kicks me out of lazy comfort mode and requires creative thinking and all my resources. Challenges can actually be fun, depending on what they are.

One key habit that has perhaps made the biggest difference in my life is the fact that I regularly challenge myself. The challenges are different depending on the stage I am in or what was happening in my life at the time. They aren't challenges that I could easily conquer. Each one started out as something I didn't think I could do. Sometimes it took me two or three attempts before I was actually able to do it. The challenges include business, health, financial and personal. None of them were achievable in less than 90 days, and some took years. The longer, harder challenges helped me grow the most.

One of the most important aspects of a healthy challenge is that the challenge is completely within your control. If you have to count on anyone else to achieve it, that's not a fair set up. Simply ask the question "Is everything within my control with this challenge?" If it is, get busy. If it's not, is there anything you can do to change that? What is fun about a challenge, especially one you didn't think you could achieve, is the feeling you get when you overcome it.

There are so many stories of people being able to do the impossible. It makes you realize that we really are responsible for limiting ourselves more than anything. Human potential to thrive is fun to see and fun to be a part of. Just think of the things in your life that have felt amazing when you have accomplished them. If you are reading this book, you are probably a reader. What have been your favorite books, fiction or non-fiction, about triumphing? Do the same thing with movies, media stories, or people you actually know.

What do you like about these stories? Are the triumphs in the same category you have been able to have victories in, or are they in areas you haven't overcome yet? If you could write your own success story, what would it be? Sometimes it's fun to just think about that a little bit. What excites you enough to do anything about it? What else might you like to try that you haven't yet? If we don't spend any time thinking about what we like or what we would like to do, we miss opportunities to do them.

You should have a fun list, and you might even want to carry it with you in case you have a few extra minutes to do something on it. Color every page in a coloring book in order, watch every episode of *The Office*, make your own root beer, try standup comedy, record each flavor of ice cream you eat, sleep outside under the stars, use a candle to make s'mores in the winter, spend a summer helping your neighborhood anonymously, challenge your kids to a Jell-O snarfing contest, while waiting for a plane make up names and stories about the people you see to entertain yourself, you get the idea.

When is the last time you had fun? If you don't know, you're in trouble. That means you don't have enough fun in your life. Each day of your life should contain at least some fun or it's not worth it. It might be only five minutes or an hour or two, but it's important. If you don't already prioritize fun, make it a new habit before you go to bed. When you end a day feeling tired and happy because you've had some fun, you know you were really alive that day.

An easy way to make sure you prioritize time for fun is to leave room for it in your schedule. We leave room for fun Thursday night. There tends to be an atmosphere for goofing around and we let Mia, Dante and Lexi stay up later. Our weekends are for fun just like a lot of families, and Sunday through Wednesday we are more disciplined with routines. Trudy, our neighbor, reserves Wednesday nights for her wine club. My mom takes painting classes on Sunday afternoons.

When I recommend leaving room in your schedule for fun, I don't just mean scheduled time for fun. To leave room for fun is also not making your schedule so tight that you don't have time to be spontaneous. We all need a little bit of breathing space which allows us to say "yes" to fleeting opportunities.

Be spontaneous if you want fun in your life.

One year at Easter, two of my nephews and a niece were going to be joining us for our annual Easter egg hunt. The cousins were all getting older and our basement seemed too easy for any real challenge in finding Easter treats. On a whim, I decided to throw the eggs and candy all over outside and in our woods. I literally ran around tossing it in every direction. The cousins had a great time hunting even harder than usual that year and enjoyed being outside for a change. But the funny part was in the spring, and even two years later, we were finding random candy under leaves or snow that had melted. Each time that happened we'd say, "Remember the year the Easter egg hunt was outside?" and laugh.

It's easy to be spontaneous with children. Can you be spontaneous on your own or with adults? For some reason, we think that's a little more risky. If that's uncomfortable for you, what are you worried about? It doesn't have to be outrageous things. It can be as simple as getting an idea and going with it before you over think it. Drive a different way to work. Try chopsticks with dinner. Go to coffee with someone you don't know. Call someone you'd like to get to know better and invite them to an event. Each of these things takes you out of your comfort zone enough to engage your senses in a new way. You don't even have to tell anyone you're doing any of these things. Just go ahead and enjoy them.

There is certainly a time and place for routines and discipline. They help us feel in control and can make tasks more efficient. They have only one shortcoming: they don't engage the imagination. Because adults have regularly engaged their imaginations we have inventions, technical advances, new genres of music, recipes, medical breakthroughs, entertainment, and joy. To use our imaginations, our minds need to be relaxed and not rigid from discipline.

Imagination at home can be re-arranging the furniture to solving an issue with your finances. It can be enjoying your deck with a refreshing drink while you just let your mind wander. Imagination can be used in planning trips, creating landscaping, dreaming, hosting parties, attracting a date, or just about anything. Getting comfortable with your imagination and using it regularly can make your life more fun and help you solve problems with ease.

Children are taught about imagination and freely use it for anything they want. Because they often receive positive feedback for it, it is seen as a good thing until adulthood. Adulthood is when we learn to hide imagination unless we are in a socially acceptable arena like being an artist. However, we are starting to see businesses and personal areas that are embracing it. Video gaming at work, playing with toys, and creative group activities are used in various industries to engage the imagination in order to innovate and solve problems. In both personal and professional life, if we want to achieve something we have never done before, we are going to have to do things we have never done before. Imagination helps you come up with new ways to go about it.

Do you have fun at work? Fun at work is not an oxymoron. It is actually a productivity tool. People who have fun at work get more done, are in a better mood and come up with more creative ideas for the company. Tons of companies from little mom-and-pop shops to large corporations understand that and use it to their advantage. When I was teaching I attended a national educators' conference where Matt Weinstein was a keynote speaker. Matt was "The Emperor" of fun (who says you have to have normal titles) for his company Playfair. Matt was promoting fun at work with his book *"Work Like Your Dog."* After the conference I read the book and created a *Have More Fun at Work* seminar. It was always a top favorite, and people talked about it for years.

With no budget and no permission, you can have more fun at work. Fun is an attitude. It is an invitation to play. You can be completely serious about your work and still go about it, at least some time, in a fun manner. To combat winter boredom and practice my creativity I'd change my voicemail everyday giving a fun tip. People started calling my phone and saying "Can you hang up and let it go to voicemail, I just wanted to hear your tip." No one can fire you for having a fun voicemail, so why are we so afraid to relax a little at work? Shenanigans are not the primary purpose of fun, and of course, you have to be mindful of that at work, but fun promotes creativity and that can mean big profit for businesses.

This last winter I got a good reminder of this. When my mom got married in October, her new husband had a three-season cabin in Minocqua, WI he wanted to sell. I was handling the building of their new home and selling each of their homes, so he wanted to know how

Lesson 9 – Having Fun!

he should deal with selling the cabin in a location that, as he described, "no one but a few snowmobilers will come by until spring." He did not know any real estate agents in the area, and wasn't interested in choosing one over the winter. After we had a good conversation about his options he decided to formally list it on the Multiple List Service (MLS) and post my real estate sign on the property, knowing that the chance of me selling it was about 5%. We figured that would at least allow the remote chance of someone seeing it to know it was for sale. In the spring I could help him find a local real estate broker.

To our surprise, we did get an offer from a local Realtor shortly before Christmas, but the terms were not in my seller's best interest and he passed on it. In February, I was spending the day with my 10-month-old niece when I got a call from a Realtor from Wausau, WI. She was leaving for California and had a "well-qualified" buyer referral for me. The referral meant she'd give me their names and it was up to me to show them the property. If they liked it I would have to see if we could make the deal work for everyone. I was excited about the possibility of making the almost impossible, possible.

Given normal circumstances like good weather, and heat when necessary, I enjoy showing houses. This time it was very important, that the buyers were well qualified as I had to drive seven hours to do this showing. The fact that Mr. Buyer was a heating and air conditioning contractor made it worth the gamble. The day of the showing it was two degrees when I left Middleton at 6:00 a.m. I needed to get there in enough time to make sure the driveway was plowed, shovel to the front steps, and plug in three space heaters and give them time to work. I knew the chances of this working were not in my favor and that the elements were against me that day. But, if I have learned anything about real estate, it is that you have to have chutzpah or you won't survive.

I made it to the cabin before the plow came through so I drudged to the door in snow up to my knees. When I managed to get the front door open with my half-frozen fingers, a blast of frigid air hit my skin and shocked me. I could see my breath, but it was so cold that rather than invisibly dissipating it just hung in the air in front of me like white gas. It felt like I was in a walk-in freezer from my days working at Hardee's. Inside, I found the space heaters, but only one would turn on. There was no way I could wait in the cabin until the showing at noon, as it was drastically colder in the cabin than outside. I headed to the gas station in town where I filled up on gas, bought another pair of gloves and called my seller to tell him the space heaters weren't working. He said, "They're from the 70s, you'll have to give them a kick." Most people would have quit right then and there. What kept me moving forward was the legal and ethical obligation I had made to sell this property for my seller.

I had no idea who the prospective buyers would be, other than a heating and air conditioning contractor and his wife. The vast majority of buyers couldn't buy a lake property when it wasn't physically possible to see what was so great about the land, Diamond Lake and the 1932 cabin itself. If I had magic I would have made it a beautiful sunny day in the middle of summer where it would be so easy for anyone to say yes. I didn't have magic so I was going to have to trust fate.

When Cindy first smiled at me and introduced

Lesson 9 – Having Fun!

herself, I knew she was a kind person and I relaxed a little. Dan came walking up next with a warm smile but, no coat. I thought *Oh, geez this isn't going to go very well* and then quickly corrected my thoughts – *he's used to working in extreme conditions.* It was too cold to talk in the cabin, so we both kept our vehicles running and met in Dan's truck. They were familiar with Diamond Lake and had a few questions. When I left their truck I wasn't sure if they were interested in buying the cabin or not (that's a smart negotiator).

On my drive back to Middleton, I had to admit that was the worst physical showing I had ever had in ten years. When I called my seller to give him feedback, he said, "Yep, I only went up there once in winter (he had owned the cabin for 33 years)." That is so typical of me or perhaps ignorant protection – that I think I can do something when I really have no idea what I'm getting myself into. Why I keep doing that is because it often works to my advantage.

Dan and Cindy Brandenburg decided to buy the cabin. My seller had owned the cabin for 33 years and his sons even had their honeymoons there. He was ready to travel, and was happy that a new family would be taking over. The Brandenburgs have three children and could also easily convert the cabin to have the modern conveniences of heat and air conditioning, so it would get more use and love throughout the year.

By the time we got to the real estate closing, my mom, Don and I knew how amazing the Brandenburgs being the new owners of the cabin was. Dan and I had each been entrepreneurs for ten years, we both had three children, and they own an RV. Somehow I had mentioned to Dan at closing that I have always wanted to take an RV trip. Without hesitation, Dan offered to let me use theirs. I was surprised by such generosity. It was easy to see their family enjoyed having fun together. Technically, all that has to happen at closing is a legal and financial transaction. When you also get a "feel good" closing, it's a rich bonus.

What was fun for me was making the seemingly impossible possible, satisfying my seller, and meeting some wonderful people who will carry on good times at the lake. It is always fun to meet good people in the world.

It's not possible for every day at work to be fun, because often work is created when people have problems they are willing to pay to be solved. However, often we can choose to be serious about what we do and also have a fun attitude while we go about it. Fun at work creates a positive energy that people notice. For most businesses fun can't be the primary focus, but it can be encouraged and enjoyed whenever it's appropriate. How can you have more fun at work?

As an author, if I have to work in an "office," my Million Dollar Office is the most fun. It has hundreds of trees, birds chirping and flying around periodically, and the full color spectrum of purples, red, oranges, yellows and greens. The sun, blue skies and rain change the mood and emotion of the space enough to engage me. The fresh air feels so luxurious and different than everywhere else. I can see for miles and it makes my imagination wander. Fiesta and Jose, my dogs, are always right at my feet and love it here as much as I do.

I can wear anything to work here, from my pajamas to my favorite outfit that my children wouldn't want me wearing in public. Bare feet, flip flops, heels or slippers are fine too. If it's cool I'll work here in a blanket, and when it's hot I can wear next to nothing. My hair is

Lesson 9 – Having Fun!

often in some highly creative concoction that I didn't check in the mirror. Make-up is never required. Music of any kind, except country and heavy metal, are accepted here. This is the kind of office you want to linger in as long as you can.

My Million Dollar Office is wide open for everyone to see and yet far enough away to be totally private. All this visual and physical stimulation are perfect for an ADHD author to write. Technically, it's my front porch. But the fun at work I have in my Million Dollar Office makes it priceless to me. I don't get to use this office all year, so it feels like a celebration on the first day of spring when I open it with two dark brown metal and wicker chairs with colorful cushions. One of my friends in Hawaii even asked me to send him a picture of me celebrating my Million Dollar Office on opening day. He appreciates my spirit of having fun at work and celebrating life.

Celebrating is one category of fun that we often overlook. We don't need to wait for bigger things to celebrate. We can celebrate several times a week or daily if we want to. What gets celebrated is purely up to us to decide. There is no committee we have to submit our request to celebrate to where they can say yes or turn us down. Good report cards often get celebrated, but what about a good test or project? They could be celebrated if you want to. What about submitting your taxes on time? That might be nice to celebrate. Do you celebrate when you have been brave enough to try something new regardless of how it ended up?

What justifies celebrating? That is completely up to you. Celebrating can be as simple as a drink to as complex as a once-in-a-lifetime trip. Blasting your favorite song can be a celebration. A mortgage burning party can be a celebration. Anything you enjoy doing can be a celebration. Firsts and lasts are great for celebrating – firsts: home, promotion, marathon, move across country, sabbatical, clutter-free room, or retreat; and lasts: daycare payment, time you have to use acne cream, report created on an old computer, time you have to use crutches, box you have to carry for a company move, sunset on vacation, and day at work before retirement. Of course, you can celebrate as often as you like for any reason you like to.

What happens when we take the time to celebrate is we get in the habit of honoring the good times. Making those moments significant also helps tone down the bad days and disappointments. When your family and friends get used to you doing this, they will start to ask you "How are you going to celebrate?" when moments in your life happen. If you encounter people who don't often celebrate, they will usually say "I never thought to celebrate that," (whatever that is). Have you ever heard of a negative celebration? I doubt it. Celebrating puts positive energy into the world, which is good for people and feels good too.

For ten years I have celebrated every house closing as a real estate broker with a new outfit. It makes me feel professional and polished, but mostly motivated to close another deal.

When people celebrate, they usually are feeling grateful for what they are celebrating. Celebrating gratitude can do amazing things in your life. Have you ever heard someone say, "The more I win the luckier I get"? That has to do with the positive energy being created when you feel gratitude. I actually make a game of keeping track of my signs of grace or winning streaks occasionally. When I write them down and take the time to acknowledge them, they put me in awe of how exciting life can be sometimes.

So if you ever thought celebrating was insignificant, you might want to take a second look at it. Celebrating can be a ton of fun and also very beneficial in your life. Celebrating, much like Living a Passionate Life!, is an attitude and way of approaching life.

If you're not having fun now, when will you be able to? Waiting to have fun is a surefire way to make sure it doesn't happen. What if having more fun was just a matter of not being so serious all the time and being more spontaneous? When is the last time you busted out dancing in your car and didn't care who saw you? Are you up for extreme fun or does that make you nervous? Is a quiet chess game fun for you, or would you rather be with 20,000 screaming fans at a sweaty concert?

Quit being shy about having fun. My friend Jason Kotecki has coined a term for this – adultitis. Adultitis occurs in adults who look completely stressed, overscheduled, always serious, with no time for shenanigans, and who truly believe fun is done with childhood. Jason used his artistic talents to create a Kim and Jason character to attract Kim's attention so they could date. In 2000 he parlayed the Kim and Jason characters into a business that "works" to escape adulthood.

People Living a Passionate Life! are having fun.

Lesson 10
Almost Heaven!

As I came to the final chapters of this book, my intuition was pulling me to Mexico. I had been there several times before, but what was probably driving the desire to get out of five long months of winter was cabin fever. I wanted to be outside in nature where I write the best without effort and feel so much gratitude.

When I decided to listen to my intuition to go to Mexico, to enjoy the finale of this book, I accepted a trip to my mom's timeshare for one final purpose – trust that the universe has got your best interest at heart. I could already see how true that was in my life living with others and traveling with companions. Last April my trip to California was about being open to people, experiences and opportunities. It seemed very fitting to end this book implementing what I'm learning about letting go and trusting the universe by traveling alone to a part of Mexico I had never been, the island of Cozumel.

Colleen has been doing my hair since 2009. I love slipping into her chair and just letting her use her expertise on length, color, and shape. Colleen is the one who added "caramel" coloring to my hair, which produced the only comment Andre has ever made about my hair: "I like the red." In the beginning, Colleen would go darker brown for the fall and winter. Andre didn't like that. For awhile, if he knew I was going to Colleen in the fall he'd say, "Make sure she keeps the red. I like the red." I think it's the spicy salsa part of red he likes, but I never asked him.

Just before I left for Cozumel, I went to Colleen. We had our usual conversation about everything that was going on in our lives. We've had some great conversations over the years. She always asks me what I'm up to or where I'm going, because I started coming to her when I was working for the multi-millionaire and had just started writing Sofia Michaels books. So I mentioned I was going to Cozumel on a solo writing trip to spend five days doing my final edits before I handed the manuscript over to my editor.

In perfect synchronicity, when I told Colleen I was flying in to Cancun, she said "Oh, so call Loomis, a car service, who will get you to the ferry that goes to Cozumel. You can even tell them what kind of drinks you want. They bring a limo and will fill it with any snacks and drinks you want. This is your sixth book. You should do that." "Okay, okay, Loomis," I said aloud to myself to help it stay in my memory. Colleen went on, "Then you should take the blue and yellow ferry. I don't remember the name but you'll see it, blue and yellow. If you have any trouble with motion sickness, the blue and yellow one seems to be better."

I was so appreciative for Colleen's specific tips as I was a little nervous about traveling alone, but I wasn't surprised that I happened to mention Cozumel to someone and she had the exact information I needed to calm my nerves. That wasn't a coincidence. It was a sign of grace, and the universe taking care of me as it always does, when I pay attention enough to notice. Remember, trust people and go with your intuition I reminded myself.

I had chosen the paperback book I would read on the plane, *The Necklace*, and I placed it on my leather chaise in our bedroom as I packed and prepared the week before. That's not my style of reading, to choose a book and wait to read it. I buy a book and immediately read the whole thing cover to cover, and rarely have multiple books going at the same time. The book I'm reading goes to bed with me at night and gets up with me for coffee in the early morning. I carry the book with me to athletic competitions, meetings, and shopping just in case I can get a few minutes to read. Over the week I would glance at *The Necklace* and knew I had to wait. Much like others feel about chocolate, I couldn't wait to get my hands on it and dive in to enjoy the pleasure I was anticipating from such an unusual book and social experiment.

The Necklace is non-fiction, as I haven't read fiction since Mia was born sixteen years ago. I figure if I'm going to spend the time to read something, I'd like to learn something as well. All I knew about *The Necklace* was what was on the cover "Thirteen women *and the* experiment *that* transformed their lives" and the fact that they had collectively bought a necklace with 118 diamonds. I was intrigued, what's the deal? I've always loved diamonds but I wouldn't jointly buy any. My first assumptions were the thirteen would be pretentious women concerned with vanity, which is not my thing. But the words "experiment" and "transformed their lives" got my interest.

Jonell McClain was the visionary who first lusted after the diamond necklace in the window of Van Grundy & Sons, a decades-old, family-owned jewelry store. I liked her creative genius to think, "I can't buy a $37,000 necklace myself, but if I could get the price down (she was a Realtor) and get eleven women to join me in the purchase, we could share it." Unrelated women, to say the least – sharing diamonds could be a major disaster! To my delight, the sweetest gesture in the deal was Mr. Van Grundy being so excited by this group of women that he negotiated that the women had to let his wife in the group, even though his wife had no interest in it. His reasoning was these women were happy, and he wanted his wife to laugh again and be a part of that group.

The main concept was about sharing and possibilities, women coming together for a common good, older women (50-62) having fun and re-inventing their lives, and being open to the unknown. In the end it added love, wisdom and generosity.

I won't wreck the story for you, but the other intriguing thing about the book is The New York Times quote on the front cover: "The best way to honor the book's principles is to share your copy with a friend." Quickly, I figured out what I would do with my copy.

When I get to Cozumel, I will find a woman who seems right for the gift and give her my copy. I liked the idea of a copy going from Middleton, Wisconsin to Cozumel, Mexico, and it would lighten my tote bag on the way back home.

The minute I come out of customs, the shuttle companies shout for your attention. I decide I have to be brave and ask "How much?" so I approach Yellow Transfers and happily pay my $32 as that was less than half-price for the companies I could have booked from home. (Sorry Colleen, I'm frugal when it doesn't really matter to me.) The lady tells me to go outside and wait for twenty minutes until more people show up for the shuttle.

I ask the first gentlemen, Alejandro, if I'm in the right place. He asks for my ticket and says "yeah, yeah, Ma'am, you have to wait. Can you wait a few minutes?" I laugh at the idea of that, as would anyone who knows me. It's clear to him I'm American. We don't wait very well. We check and re-check and want to keep moving this, whatever this is, forward. I thank him and remind myself that I have to trust people here.

A few minutes later Julio looked at me and perhaps he saw the frown wrinkle right between my eyes that my mom has warned me about since fifth grade. He says, "Ma'am, no worries. No worries. It's time to relax." A smile comes to my face as I remember exactly why my intuition told me to come to Mexico as the finale of this book – to slow down, celebrate and savor life.

I had the presence of mind to ask for a garbage bag at the Miami hotel before I left. In general I'm very low maintenance, but I had just gotten a new orange leather tote that was carrying my laptop and camera that I didn't want to ruin. While I was standing and

Lesson 10 – Almost Heaven!

waiting for the shuttle, it started to sprinkle. The clear garbage bag didn't look classy but I didn't care. I had learned a very important travel tip from my sister Diana when we were 12 and 13. We had a ten-hour ride each way to visit our grandparents, so we had to be creative in the car to entertain ourselves. We looked in the back of the station wagon and saw luggage tags, lots of luggage tags. Diana had long hair and I spent over an hour braiding her hair like Bo Derrick, using the elastic from the luggage tags to tie each braid.

When it came time to get out at a gas station to go to the bathroom, I looked at Diana and said "I'm sorry. Do you want me to take them out?" Diana didn't hesitate a second and replied "I will never see these people again. I don't care," and off she went into the gas station. "You'll never see these people again," became our brave travel motto to go ahead and be silly. The garage bag luggage reminds me to relax and be silly. Nothing is that serious when you are on vacation.

The shuttle takes me to Playa del Carmen, where I can get a ferry to Cozumel. The ferry was straight ahead of me one block. I could see the ocean and as I scanned around, there were tons of color and beautiful shops. When the driver lets me off, I can't help myself. At the corner where I was dropped off I see security guards and then notice it was a diamond store, one of my original lusts. I started snapping pictures and walking down the long alley of shops. When I see an even larger International Diamond store with four security guards, I didn't hesitate to snap a picture. Then I notice one of the guards waving his arm and hear him calling "Miss, Miss!" "Oh, no photos" I say and he says "Si, no photos." I holler, "Lo siento (sorry)" and quickly walk on.

Living a Passionate Life!

After I get almost to the end of the shops I decided to turn around to eat at the restaurant I saw near the ferry. I can't read most of the menu so I decide to have my usual, steak fajitas and a Corona. I tell the waiter and he says something I can't understand. I said "pardon?" He repeats it and I still didn't understand but my intuition was – it's too early. I thought it was noon or maybe even two o'clock as I had lost track of time with no real responsibilities but to keep track of my carry-on and tote bag. "Too early?" I say. "Yes, too early." He gently smiles at me and says, "Maybe a Coke (He means a Pepsi – they call everything a Coke)?" "Yes, a Coke" I respond. He says okay and walks away. Less than two minutes later, he comes back and says "Okay, you want to order now?" I don't get this game we're playing, but I say, "Yes, steak fajitas and..." He finishes with "a Corona?" I hesitate with a weak and slow "yes?" He tells me "Yes, it is time", with a big smile on his face.

My three years of high school Spanish were long since helpful. As he looks away I check the time on my cell phone. It was 10 a.m.! Embarrassed and laughing, I realize I just ordered my earliest Corona ever and made my second oops in Mexico. When Miguel came back to the table he said "You're on vacation. You're in Mexico. It's time to have fun, yes?" As I'm leaving I see a fruit, yogurt and granola platter that would have been more appropriate, but as my teenagers would say, "YOLO, Mom!"

As I sit waiting for the ferry to Cozumel, I feel just fine being by myself. There is nice music playing at the thatched bar on the beach with a beach massage station with five massage tables – $20 for 70 minutes. A massage on the beach was going to be my guilty pleasure while I'm here, but at that price, I don't even have to feel bad.

My mind next goes to thinking about the various things I've written so far in Living a Passionate Life! I knew I'd figure out what "Almost Heaven" even means when I got here. To this point I just thought it was a great chapter title, and it wraps up the introduction where I told you I saw the street sign "Almost Heaven" in Hot Springs, Virginia. Although I also knew there was a reason I saw that sign.

Almost Heaven is the joys in life as much as it is your life right now in this moment as you are Living a Passionate Life! But it is also the lessons I've learned about life so far at 45. As I read what I just wrote, that feels right. This is a profound life experience, and it is almost heaven if we make the most of it. If you didn't enjoy the journey and take full advantage of it, you have no one to blame.

When I arrive at my mom's timeshare, The Allegro, they say "Oh, you are an owner?" I shyly say "Well, my mom is." He tells me "They will come get you with a golf cart – one moment." After that I am whisked off to a private clubhouse where they greet me with champagne, explain to me the amenities for owners, and deliver me to my private room. It's perfect. There is a hammock on the front porch, two wicker chairs, and a table for writing. Inside there is a beautiful king size bed with reading lights, a stocked wet bar with full bottles of Jim Beam whiskey, Borzoi vodka and Bacardi rum (I rarely cheat on my Captain Morgan, but perhaps I will), a bistro table and two more chairs stained in espresso brown, and a full bathroom with a modern tiled shower and a large rectangle sink with no real sides on it, so the water splashes all over.

As I quickly put my things away and go look around

Living a Passionate Life!

the resort, it is perfect. Tons of beautiful palm trees and tropical greenery, pools, hot tubs, restaurants, a beachfront bar, a beach massage hut, activity center, dive school, tennis courts, sports bar, children's pool, adult pool, and of course a long stretch of oceanfront. It is an all-inclusive resort, so there is more than plenty of food and drink any time you wish for it. This is just as my mom had wanted for me, a fantasy writing getting away for an author who is really married with three children and businesses to run. I greatly appreciate this generous priceless gift from her. She has always encouraged creativity.

As I start to walk on the beach with my feet submerged to my ankles, I relax and take in the light breeze, sunshine and aqua blue colors of the ocean. I realize several Americans warned me to stay on the resort, so I decide I'm safe walking to the pier of the next resort and back. Okay, you caught me with a goal again, but the longer I walk the more I relax.

As I look at the sea shells I can't help but think of my children. We collect shells and sand from each beach we go to in a clear water bottle and display them in our guest room. When I stop for a few minutes to look at the ocean straight on, a wave of emotions comes over me as I think about how incredibly miniscule we each are. It's not sadness, but rather humbling to consider the magnitude of the world and what that means. Of course, it reminds me of the comment that "we are all connected," and that is so true as everyone here wants to experience joy, eat, drink, and take care of their families. There is no color or kind to that.

When I return to the resort I tried to lie on a chair and sit still in the sun. Maybe twenty minutes went by, that included lying on my back and front, and I had to

Lesson 10 – Almost Heaven!

do something different. When I was a teenager I use to worship the sun with baby oil, tanning blankets and Sun In. That makes me laugh when I remember the first time my mom brought Diana and I to Mexico as teenagers some 30 years ago. I had gotten so dark brown and was practicing Spanish with someone in line at the airport. Security stopped me from getting on the plane since they didn't think I belonged to my lighter-skinned mother (It was 1984.) I had no identification since I didn't drive yet. They held me while several men talked to my mom. I knew in that moment if she couldn't make them understand I wouldn't be leaving Mexico with her and Diana.

Minutes later, they all returned to me smiling and said I may go. That was just one of many times I saw my mom do whatever it takes. Where do you think I got my chutzpah? Now that I've come to my senses, I enjoy being out in the sun yet more in the shade. Mexico and this timeshare are a part of my mom's legacy she wanted us to have.

At dinner that evening, I was a table for one. For some reason that makes people uncomfortable as they said "Oh, I'm sorry, Bella," – although I felt perfectly happy. This trip wasn't a family or couple's vacation for me. It was a solace time of reflection and evaluation of my life and the book so far. How many people do that to this extent? I had bent to please people a little by bringing my writing bag along as my companion, but I didn't personally need it.

The food was ridiculously abundant, and I had promised Dante I would take a picture of every food item that was there. Camera in hand, I snapped pictures of all the food, which got an odd reaction from people devouring the food stations. If I felt uncomfortable, I just said, "My son wants to see all of the food as he is taking Spanish (Thank you Dante for the diversion.)" Everything was delicious, especially the jumbo garlic shrimp, which Andre would never smell on my breath.

As I have said earlier, one thing I always notice when I take time to reflect is how much fear controls so much of our decisions and life experiences. It's true of me as well, if I don't push myself past it. It's easier to say no and stay in our comfort zones, where we slowly diminish until we find ourselves just sitting on the couch at home.

When I ask myself the age-old question "What's the worst that can happen?" and think about any "worst" that could have happened, compared to what actually did happen, it's not much. While there were one or two decisions that caused me heartache for a while, in the scheme of things that just added to who I am today, so it's all good in the end.

How do you let fear control the decisions and experiences you have in life? I'm not advocating the kind of *Eat, Pray, Love* where you dump your marriage and children and take off to anywhere you please. But I am talking about how the excuses we give for why we can't do something are often just that – excuses. If you are a citizen from a free country, you have the right to live your life even if it's intertwined with others. What you'll find is the more you stop fear from controlling your decisions and experiences the freer you will be. If your heart gets racing you simply remind yourself "everything is fine right now" because chances are at this very moment you are fine if your hair's not on fire.

When I was flying to Miami, Florida to get a connecting flight to Cozumel, we couldn't land. There was bad weather and turbulence so severe they eventually closed the Miami airport and kept us in a holding pattern for over an hour. At first I got a little nervous, thinking I would miss my connecting flight, but then I eavesdropped on the flight attendant explaining to another passenger what was happening. I heard blah, blah, something, and then – "the airport is closed, all flight have been cancelled." I recognized there was nothing I could do, and accepted the situation.

But when we landed we are all sent to re-booking, and I started getting nervous about not wanting a later flight that would get me to Playa del Carmen so late I might miss the last ferry at 11 p.m. (which was actually 10 p.m. – so much for correct details) and find myself in the dark and homeless for the night. I felt sick to my stomach from the turbulence and maybe the fear story I was playing in my head.

I texted Andre just to let him know I was stuck in Miami and didn't know what was going to happen until I got through re-booking. Waiting in line, there were certainly people flipping out with F-bombs and a mom on the phone going off on her son for skipping school that day while she took off on a plane to somewhere. People get ugly when they are tired, angry, or frustrated.

I was trying to control my stomach from thinking it constantly needed to go to the bathroom so I could wait my turn in the long winding line up to re-booking. It was already dark so my plans were going to change in the dark no matter what I did. Just breathe, I told myself – you have money, a credit card, a debit card and cash, you'll be fine. When I finally get my turn the man tells me I have been re-booked at 7:55 a.m. which meant I had to be back at the airport at 3:55 a.m. for an international flight. I would be staying at the Comfort Inn with a shuttle waiting for me downstairs. Okay, not my first choice, but there was nothing I could do but accept it. My stomach settled down as I wouldn't be homeless in the dark alone. When I called Andre we agreed it was for the best, and I'd try again tomorrow.

If we let little bumps in the road detour us we won't get very far. There are plenty of people in life stuck in a rut on the side of the road complaining to anyone who will listen. I don't want to be one of them. I want to keep calm and carry on, as the famous British saying goes. Just like everyone else I do get scared of what I imagine I can't do and then I tell myself the truth. *Right now you are fine and if you really want to, you will find a way.* It has been that way my whole life.

The first morning on Cozumel I'm awake at 3 a.m. This isn't a total surprise because I often do that at home, too. Here I have no responsibilities, no schedule and had plenty of sleep, so I was ready to go. I turned on the television to find very few English channels and they were bad English at that. I ended up reading and putzing around my room until 5 a.m., when coffee was served at the main dining room.

I slowly opened my door to pitch black darkness. I closed the door and checked the clock on my cell phone again in case I have the time wrong. Nope. It was 5 a.m. and there were no lights on outside. No building lights, no lights on the paths, no lights. One of my favorite things is coffee right when I get up. I enjoy it while I'm reading or writing. This is a new day, a new adventure, so I decide to use the light on my cell phone to help me make my way to the main building to get coffee.

Somewhat lost in the dark on a path to somewhere

Lesson 10 – Almost Heaven!

on a chilly morning reminded me of summer camp. For some reason I was staying to the right edge of the stone path and winding my way to what I thought was the right direction. I looked up and saw a man standing in the middle of the path with white hair, an open button-down short-sleeve shirt, shorts and no shoes. He asked me what time it was. I told him it was about 5 a.m. and said I was going to get coffee. He said that is what he was doing too. We both laughed about being up too early. I could tell right away he was a friendly jokester. We chatted a bit and I told him this trip was the end of my book. After we got our coffee, we each went off on a different dark path to wherever.

Hours later I ran into him again by the pool. This time I could see he did in fact have brilliant white hair, a deep tan and a lady with dark hair sitting next to him. They were both very kind and asked me how my book was coming along as we ran into each other throughout the week. Actually, he liked to tease, "Are you done yet?" and I had to tell him I was making myself linger so I could enjoy the experience until I was leaving Cozumel. Otherwise I'd have nothing to do for days. He laughed. I would guess both of them to be in their sixties, but it really didn't matter here.

Later that day, 80s tunes are cranking from the activities desk, like "Highway to Hell" by AC/DC, and "Glory Days" by Bruce Springsteen. It's funny, I still remember all of the lyrics like it was yesterday. I can't help myself, my feet are dancing and I don't even care as I bang away on my laptop, chewing gum. No one seems to care. A little Bob Marley comes on, which is perfect for the lounge chair I'm in overlooking the ocean.

Two ladies get my attention and make me laugh.

Living a Passionate Life!

One is a mom in a bikini over 40 – don't ask, you can just tell. But what's great about her is she is playing ping pong over the volleyball net in the sand with her son who appeared to be about four. When she managed to hit one over that he couldn't return, she does a gleeful dance. Beating her son wasn't what was great. The fact that she was just happy and didn't care if anyone saw it was great. Then I notice another woman off to the side of the volleyball court who was really getting into the music with her cheetah bikini, white sheer cover up with long sleeves and open front, and dark sunglasses who was gyrating something fierce all by her bad self. Amen sister, enjoy yourself!

I decide to go to the in-pool bar for one margarita before lunch. There is one bar seat open with a woman sitting next to it and a man, whom I presumed to be her husband, standing behind her. As I step into the pool to take the seat I respond to the bar tender "a margarita, plain, please." The woman sitting next to me asks "What did you call it?" I said "Plain, I meant original but for some reason I couldn't think of that. I have no idea where that came from" I tell her. We all three laugh.

The man was in fact her husband, and the three of us had a wonderful conversation about our lives and our families. Her husband did a good job of not shying away as we talked. We talked for quite a while and when I was getting ready to leave I flippantly said "Do you read?" She knew what I meant and told me she had just run out of books to read and needed something new. I asked her if she had read *The Necklace* to which she responded with a "no." I quickly explained the premise of the book and asked if she'd like to have it. She accepted. I was pleasantly pleased as we both said

"Must have been meant to be."

The next day, again at noon, I proceed to the in-pool bar for my one margarita before lunch. The same woman is there, by herself this time. I learn her name is Melissa and her husband is Dennis. As I get my drink and we quickly get right back into conversation, I think it's so great that adults welcome you in just like preschool when you're the new kid. Before I know it we've started a party as Dennis joins us and Edwin puts another margarita next to me. "Oh, you're trouble Edwin" I tell him. Edwin counters back with "No. Not me, it's him (pointing at Dennis)." Another couple from Canada sees us at the bar and teases me by saying "Now are we going to be in the book? When does the movie come out?" "Yes, come on, join us!" I say back to him. Then Melissa is happy to see Karen and her husband, who I also met yesterday, and they come join us. Dennis decides everyone needs a Kahlua shot, and orders them for everyone. The trouble with all-inclusive resorts is that all of the alcohol and food is included, so it's easy to indulge. We laughed so many times and the time just got away from all of us.

Melissa and I agreed we needed the same greasy cheeseburger just like each of us had yesterday. She and her husband Dennis invited me to join them in the pool restaurant for lunch, which I did. All I put on my plate was the greasy cheeseburger with ketchup, mustard and 15 pickles, without all the extra side dishes I had yesterday. This cheeseburger wasn't as good as Andre's off our grill, but it was a wonderful cheeseburger. After lunch, I mentioned I was going to the resort next door to check it out as it was another timeshare my family could go to, and Melissa and Dennis decided to join me.

We walked along the beach until we arrived at a more secluded resort covered by beachfront, pools and lush greenery you couldn't even see through. This resort was more for adults and honeymooners; we only saw one child. There were stone paths with water fountains that led to the main lobby building and I asked to see a two-bedroom unit so I could take pictures for my mom and sister. Melissa and Dennis were great sports as they said "We have nothing else to do" and they were willing to wait for me to do this one task. When we walked back to our resort I realized I had lost my key from my camera case that was open while I was taking pictures. Again, Melissa and Dennis went with me to the First Club where timeshare owners got service. I got another key – which I proceeded to leave on my bed when I shut the door to go to dinner. Good Lord!

So I had intended to have one margarita, and instead I had two and a shot of Kahlua, misplaced two keys and never wrote another thing that day. But I had a good time and had met more people who just wanted to have a good time and enjoy this island experience we were all on. Normally I'm an intelligent person. I keep a schedule and am ever the consummate professional. Really, this was another example of the fact that I have two modes, 100 miles per hour or asleep. I had hit vacation mode and my brain was turned off. All of my usual responsibilities were well cared for at home, thousands of miles away. I was on a safe island with couples and families and security available all over. But more importantly, people were so freely willing to include me. It was fun.

There is magic in the all-inclusive resorts. There is no competition. Everything from food, drinks, alcohol, and beach towels to seating is abundant. People are happy to get you a drink or give you their chair. It is share and share alike, because there is plenty, rather than every man for himself. People act different in this environment. The first few days I'd guess people overindulge. Yet within a few days they are probably back to their normal amount of food and drink since they know it won't disappear, or perhaps even less as they tire of the same offerings over and over again. Granted, people are on vacation, but the all-inclusive aspect relaxes people even further into abundant mentality which is so nice for a change.

Of course, this isn't realistic in capitalistic countries where competition is a lifestyle choice in the game of survival of the fittest. Certainly there are aspects of competition that are necessary, yet I've learned my only real competition in life is myself. I will never have the same skills, timing, opportunities, or resources as anyone else. The best way for me to compete is against myself for my personal best. If I'm not happy with the results I am getting, it's up to me to find a way to change that. I am accountable.

This approach also takes away the envy or frustration about other people as you only focus on yourself as to what is going well and what needs to change. I'd say it has been about a decade since I've changed to my only true competition is with myself for my personal best. With that attitude, I've been able to shape myself and my life to be what I've always wanted it to be. So I can say it has worked for me. My work ethic is a strength that has always stood out, and when I think of the Mexican culture, it has a very hard-working mentality, too.

The Mexican people are beautiful people. They are so

physically hard working, they respect their heritage and honor family, and they have found a way to make their culture their livelihood. Christian was the host at the restaurant who, the next day, was also the activities director. That's what's funny about these resorts. You will see one person do about five different jobs. I was sitting on a swing at the bar writing when Christian stopped by to see how my book was coming along. I am always intrigued by people, and since he had a few minutes I asked if he had always lived on this island. He explained to me that he originally came from Puerta Vallarta about four months ago and will be done with his job here in about a week because it is the slow season. I couldn't help asking "What will you do?" He said, "I don't know. That is how it is here for so many. We get laid off and there are few jobs off the resorts. The men with families get the jobs first because most of the women stay home with the children. I don't have any children yet so, I don't know."

The mom in me was concerned for a bit thinking about what that must be like and how do you deal with it. Christian was being very open so I said "And when you came from Puerta Vallarta, how did you get your stuff here? That had to be hard." He explained to me that he took just essentials like sheets and what would fit in his duffel bag. Then he came here on the ferry and had to find work to get food and a place to stay. I can't even fathom that. In Mexico, just like plenty of other areas of the world, you have to go where the jobs are.

What Christian told me just confirms my awe of the power of the human spirit. We hear stories every day of people in horrendous situations that you think would break them, and somehow they make it through. We hear children are resilient. But really humans are incredibly resilient and when you ever need a little more strength just look to these kinds of people and their stories. They are inspiring.

That second day I got more comfortable with my rudeness of bringing my laptop to breakfast. I would just flash it a little bit to Benito when he'd come get me for seating. He's said, "Ah, yes, I have the perfect seat for you." He'd take me to a cozy spot out of the way of the main dining area where my typing wouldn't annoy anyone. It was tucked in a corner where I see everyone coming to the dining hall, and overlooked the area where people went to the bar in the evening and coffee in the morning.

For several mornings there was an older gentlemen eating to my right all by himself – the only other person I noticed eating alone. On my last morning, as he was walking away he turned around and walked back to me. "I have to ask, what you are doing? I've wondered all week," he said. When I told him he said, "I wish I had asked you earlier. I have to go scuba diving, but that's so interesting." It made me happy, because I knew I was on to something with this book.

In the evening I'd take a small notebook for dinner because once the ideas start popping, as they will do in fresh air, ocean breezes, palm trees, and quiet, I need to capture them by jotting them down before they are wasted. That is one of the greatest ways I've learned to respect creativity. It can come from something you see, hear, feel or just come to you at any time whether you are ready or not. That's probably one of my best benefits of always carrying an iPhone – I can quickly jot down a thought. I'm sure people were wondering what I was up to, but I have learned to not care and also get a little thrill out of leaving them wondering.

After I had been there a few days I was busy banging away on my laptop on a lounge chair overlooking the ocean when an old lady interrupted my train of thought with "Can't leave your work, can you? That's the trouble with people today. They always gotta have their hands on computers and stuff." Her tone was harsh and biting. I could tell by looking at her she was one of those people who complains on vacation and probably about her medical conditions, as she was rubbing her feet while she made that comment to me. Because of that I gave her the two-second explanation – I'm here working, this isn't a vacation. She proceeded to tell me her whole family was taking a scuba lesson and she had to just wait for them. She went on about random negativity, constantly interrupting me, and I knew she was the kind of creative buzzkill that would ruin the whole experience of what I was doing there, so I packed up and changed writing spots.

Later that night when I sat in the hammock for the first time with nothing in my hands (I always have a book or something to do – I can't even watch TV without at least one more thing to do) and I was looking around at how peaceful everything looked, I thought about what the lady had said: "Can't leave your work, can you?" Maybe the truth is it annoyed me a little because it was essentially true. I have never been one to sit still. Ever since I had children, I hate to waste time. There's always something to do. She prompted me to linger in the hammock a little longer, walk down by the vendors and entertainment that was brought in by the pool, and just reflect on when I "don't work." Given what I do, real estate and writing, I work on and off all the time. It has become a strong habit and for the most part I don't think it hurts anyone, although I get comments about it.

Something I've contemplated more than work is my constant need to be working on a goal or moving forward. My friend Pierce calls this striving. Wayne Dyer's movie *The Shift* talks about the literal shift from striving to meaning in life. I do get that, and am past the point where I don't need to strive for stuff, titles, etc. The way Wayne Dyer explains meaning in life is the same as when I explained what a profound experience life is. But where there is an uncomfortable method variance for me is meaning in life for Wayne doesn't include goals or us directing anything. It means letting life unfold the way it wants to. "Surrender and allow" is his primary attitude. I have been able to do that, with a lot of effort, when I really work at it. Yes, that is an oxymoron for a type A personality. To be specific, I have done it twice for one month and once for three months, but I have not been able to adopt it as a constant way of being.

What is more typical for me is a hybrid approach. I certainly do make more of an effort to relax each day, try to surrender after I've put all the effort I can into something, enjoy my life more, realize I am co-creating my life, and respect the profound experience life is. I would not be who I am without high energy and striving. People make all sorts of comments when I am subdued on purpose. I certainly have changed more to the "being" rather than "doing" in the Be-Do-Have model. I will always be an active student in life. I want to learn as much as life has to teach me, and make a difference by inspiring others to do the same.

Really, as I lounge in my hammock on my last night in Cozumel, before I return home to my full life, I realize for the first time in my life that I feel satisfied. As I think over my entire life so far, from where I come from to where I am at today, I am pleased by how it's turned out. That might not sound too significant to you, perhaps as boring as plain toast, but for me to realize I feel satisfied is like seeing the first flowers of spring. It feels exciting and fragile, like gorgeous blue robin's eggs, and wonderful. Perhaps there's a hint of dopamine with a new thrill of your life looking different in a good way.

Maybe it's easiest to understand that I was an A student in college. Type A, A students are rarely satisfied because they always feel they could have done something better. But when they finally have that experience of not just feeling good, but feeling satisfied, it fills a void that use to drive them and makes them feel complete.

There are two areas I have probably grown in the most this year that I didn't even expect when I started this journey. I thought I would enjoy myself a little more, live a little bigger and hopefully inspire myself and others to more than seize their lives. Yet as I looked at life in general and people's lives in particular, it started to change me. The first main area of growth was respect for people. When it comes all the way down to it for every human being, as I had mentioned earlier, they want to experience joy, have their basic needs met, and take care of their families. When you look even deeper into their eyes you can see they each want to be loved and know that someone really sees them and acknowledges their existence. When you go all the way to that level it doesn't matter if the person is male or female, colored or not, speaks a different language, dresses like you or not, young or old, loud or quiet, gentle or rough, pessimistic or optimistic. That is amazing.

The second main area of growth was spiritual. When I started writing this book, I wanted to challenge myself as a writer. I made a commitment to let intuition help me write this book instead of the usual pre-decided chapters and outlines. I had to trust faith more than control. I had to let the book write itself more than I dictated. There were times when the book seemed to get much deeper than I was comfortable publically saying, as I have always been private about my spirituality. Just as there were times when I had no idea where the book was going or what I was going to say about it. It was a completely different writing experience, a much easier and more enjoyable one, than ever before. It strengthened my faith and gratitude and certainly increased my joy.

A spontaneous laugh and smile came to my face as I realize this book was written just like the ocean. A big tide of excitement started my passion to write the first lesson. Then, halfway through lesson two, I lost steam and came rolling back to shore not sure where to go next. After a while I got an inspiration for a topic that became a lesson, but I had no idea where it should go, and off I went again. When you are out a ways, the flow of water is not always straight. It shifts and moves to make a beautiful awe of nature.

Lessons were not written linearly. One would take off in one direction, and my next lesson idea would need to go lessons away from the last one I wrote. Two or three times, as I have mentioned, a lesson would take off in a totally different direction mid-stream. When it was all done, it turned out I wrote lesson one, half of lesson two, lesson five, lesson eight, lesson four, lesson three, lesson six, lesson nine, lesson seven, lesson ten, finished lesson two, dumped lesson ten and re-wrote it.

Living a Passionate Life!

When the order was established, I just made sure the end of the previous chapter blended with the next. If you aren't ADHD or intuitive that might drive you nuts, but I had made a commitment to challenge myself as a writer and passion and Living a Passionate Life! is often not linear. Passion is energy that ebbs and flows and take off in directions of its own, just like the ocean. When I take on a challenge, I attack it with a fierce fire in my belly until I achieve it.

This is the third Sofia Michaels book. They are more powerful than any other personal development technique I've ever done. While someone else might not go to this length to learn from and capture their life like this – it has become one of my passions.

While I'm packing up my things, with the front door open Daniel shouted his usual question, "Are you done yet?" as he and Patricia came up the path towards my door. This time I said a calm and confident *"Yes."* Daniel and Patricia came by to say good-bye. That was so nice of them. That's how you know if you matter to people, when they go out of their way to acknowledge you. I gave them a quick tour of my writing hut and they asked what's next for me. I explained that I'm not sure yet. I was going home, and we'd have to see what happens. We agreed it was wonderful meeting each other and we wished each other well. Just as I had believed, there are good people all over in the world.

When they left, I put my suitcase and bag by the front door so I could say goodbye to Cozumel and the resort. I walked down the path towards the pool and ocean. The sun was bright, but not too hot. There was a nice breeze, and I closed my eyes for a minute to take it all in. This has been a wonderful experience. I opened my eyes and walked further towards the ocean in the

Lesson 10 – Almost Heaven!

direction I would be traveling on the ferry soon. The ocean is always so amazing and mighty no matter where you experience it. But the colors of the ocean and sand are always different.

Next, I wanted to give a larger tip to each of the people who had served me this week to show my gratitude. Each time I received service I tipped them, but today's large tip was unexpected and therefore a nice surprise. I walked to the pool house to give Juan the tip. He was a teenager and beamed when I gave it to him. "Thank you, Señora. Thank you very much," he said. I replied with "I appreciate your help all week." Benito and two other servers were next. After that I found Christian, and finally left a nice tip in my room for housekeeping. This was a gratitude exercise, as I have certainly learned that gratitude is key to Living a Passionate Life!

I got my luggage and walked to the main lobby, where I asked them to call me a taxi. The lady told me to go outside and they would call me a taxi. That seemed a little odd to me as I hadn't noticed a phone outside at the service stand. I walked up to the stand and said "Will you please call me a taxi?" Pancho says "You want a taxi?" "Yes, please" I tell him. He literally waved his right arm up and down once. I see a car pull out of the parking lot directly across the street. I laugh and say, "Oh, I see. 'Call' a taxi." The man is proud, with his beaming smile facing me. That's what I love about Mexico – it's fun.

And as I prepare to leave Cozumel, Adolfo takes my suitcase. "Bella, you come back home soon, yes?" I know I will, and hopefully I'll bring my family with me. As I drive away in the taxi I feel a wave of emotion wash over me. My delicious book is complete – a bittersweet ending on a book I have loved. I'm more than satisfied with my life and I am going back to my family, my greatest love. I can certainly say I am Living a Passionate Life! and it feels good.

Photography Credits

Foreplay!	Tammy Haverkampf of Haver North Photography
Living a Passionate Life!	Andre Michaels
Living a Dirty Life!	Andre Michaels
Living La Vida Loca!	Social Michaels
Experiencing Life!	Anonymous passerby
Make it a Great Day!	Sofia Michaels
Passion Workers!	Dante Michaels
Parenting Legacy!	Steve Fermanich
Having Fun!	Dave Rassmussen
Almost Heaven!	Sofia Michaels
Front cover	Terry Healy Lemke
Back cover	Dante and Lexi Micheals
Author	Catherine of Catherine Baldauf Photography

Acknowledgement

My greatest gratitude is for my family, who supports my writing and graciously allows me to write about our life together. That's an amazing gift from a growing family that I will always treasure. Sofia Michaels' books have become the scrapbooks of my life that I will use to reminisce when I am an old woman and reflect on what an amazing life I have lived.

Specifically, my mom Pillar and I have transitioned to a new aspect of our soul mate relationship as artists who encourage each other. It's precious to have someone who understands this crazy desire to create even when it's messy and not easy. But most importantly, she is someone I can show each finished piece who knows this is how I honored my gifts from God.

Cindia Chau-Boon, you were the encouragement to put this book together. For a year in our mastermind group, you kept telling me to put a product together that allowed people to see how I live and think. That encouragement eventually became this book.

I would like to thank intuition for playing with me during the writing of this book. As you know, I couldn't do it without you. This has been the most fun book to write because of you. You have an open invitation to show up in my life every day.

Kristen Allen, my editor, you were a godsend. At first I couldn't understand why I had two failed editors on this book. But of course, intuition brought Rich Greene back into my life to remind me to take a leap and trust Fiverr.com. You are smart, professional, responsive, and thorough. You cared about this book and my success with it. You polished my art, and I sincerely thank you for that.

There were also countless passionate people who were brave enough to talk about their passions with me. I appreciate each conversation and probing question. But most of all, I am grateful that you allow people into your life with open arms. We all get better when people share themselves. As you know by now, I have a deep need for emotional connection and you connected deeply without feeling any of it was provocative or intrusive. Someday, maybe, that will be the social norm.

About the Author

Sofia Michaels, M.S. Education

After writing two personal branding books as a teacher and life coach, Sofia turned those skills on herself.

The result was a cathartic experience for her, and an affordable coaching tool for her readers. Her first Sofia Michaels book was a memoir to overcome her past. Then, when she asked herself where she needed to grow next, the result was *Pretendia: Smash the Glass Slipper and Awaken Your Best Self*. And finally, *Living a Passionate Life!* completes the Sofia Michaels Launch Trilogy.

Sofia Michaels is the broker/owner of Storylane Properties and a former high school and college marketing teacher. She has been a keynote and seminar presenter for 28 years, as well as a tele-class presenter and forum moderator. She is also the creator and owner of Street Smart Publishing.

Sofia lives in Middleton, Wisconsin with her

husband, three children and two dogs.

*Author works under Sheri Fermanich & Sofia Michaels brands – they are two different voices. The 1st is all business and the 2nd is spicier and all about life.

www.ingramcontent.com/pod-product-compliance
Lightning Source LLC
Chambersburg PA
CBHW071305110426
42743CB00042B/1177